THOMAS M[...]

D0255544

Utopia

EDITED BY

GEORGE M. LOGAN

AND

ROBERT M. ADAMS

CAMBRIDGE
UNIVERSITY PRESS

Published by the Press Syndicate of the University of Cambridge
The Pitt Building, Trumpington Street, Cambridge CB2 1RP
40 West 20th Street, New York, NY 10011–4211, USA
10 Stamford Road, Oakleigh, Melbourne 3166, Australia

The translation of *Utopia* used in this edition is based on
The Norton Critical Edition of *Utopia* by Sir Thomas More,
translated and edited by Robert M. Adams.
Copyright © 1975 by W. W. Norton & Company, Inc.
By permission of W. W. Norton & Company, Inc.

© in the introduction and other new material
Cambridge University Press 1989

First published 1989
Reprinted 1991, 1992, 1993, 1995, 1996

Printed in Great Britain by Athenæum Press Ltd, Gateshead, Tyne & Wear

British Library cataloguing in publication data

More, *Sir* Thomas, *Saint, 1478–1535*
Utopia.
1. Utopia – Early works
I. Title   II. Logan, George M.
III. Adams, Robert M.
321′07

Library of Congress cataloguing in publication data

More, Thomas, Sir, Saint, 1478–1535.
Utopia.
(Cambridge texts in the history of political thought)
Translated from the Latin.
Bibliography.
Includes index.
1. Utopias.
I. Logan, George M.
II. Adams, Robert M.
III. Title.
IV. Series.
HX810.5.E54   1988
335′.02′   88–25660

ISBN 0 521 34573 1 hardback
ISBN 0 521 34797 1 paperback

CAMBRIDGE TEXTS IN THE
HISTORY OF POLITICAL THOUGHT

MORE
Utopia

CAMBRIDGE TEXTS IN THE HISTORY OF POLITICAL THOUGHT

Series editors

RAYMOND GEUSS *Columbia University*
QUENTIN SKINNER *Christ's College, Cambridge*
RICHARD TUCK *Jesus College, Cambridge*

The series is intended to make available to students the most important texts required for an understanding of the history of political thought. The scholarship of the present generation has greatly expanded our sense of the range of authors indispensable for such an understanding, and the series will reflect those developments. It will also include a number of less well-known works, in particular those needed to establish the intellectual contexts that in turn help to make sense of the major texts. The principal aim, however, will be to produce new versions of the major texts themselves, based on the most up-to-date scholarship. The preference will always be for complete texts, and a special feature of the series will be to complement individual texts, within the compass of a single volume, with subsidiary contextual material. Each volume will contain an introduction on the historical identity and contemporary significance of the text concerned.

For a list of titles published in the series, please see end of book.

For Cathy

Contents

Acknowledgements

The editors are grateful to Quentin Skinner and Richard Tuck for valuable comments on the penultimate version of the Introduction, and to Ruth Sharman, whose careful reading of the edition on behalf of the Press prompted a number of corrections and improvements. David Barnard, Catherine Harland and Charles and Carol Molson read all or part of earlier versions of the edition and offered many good suggestions. Karen Donnelly has provided help of various kinds.

We are indebted to John Benedict for securing the blessing of W. W. Norton & Company on a project that involved recasting the translation of *Utopia* that Adams had published with Norton. For the present edition, Adams recast the translation and made new translations of some of the ancillary letters and poems. Logan provided the introductory materials and the annotations. Each editor read the other's work and made innumerable suggestions for changes in it.

G.M.L.

R.M.A.

Notes on the text

(1) *Documentation*. The paraphernalia of documentation have been kept to a minimum. Publication data for some standard works are given in Suggestions for further reading: in the footnotes, these works are cited only by author and title. With the exceptions noted in Suggestions for further reading, all citations of classical works are to the editions of the Loeb Classical Library. Neither editors' names nor publication data are given for these editions. References to the Bible are to the King James Version – except for the Apocrypha, where references are to the Vulgate.

(2) *Abbreviations*. CW = Yale *Complete Works of St Thomas More*; CWE = Toronto *Collected Works of Erasmus*.

(3) *Names*. Names of historical figures of More's era are spelled as in *Contemporaries of Erasmus: A Biographical Register of the Renaissance and Reformation*. The sole exception is Pieter Gillis, for whom we use the familiar anglicised form Peter Giles.

(4) *Modernisation*. Whenever sixteenth-century English is quoted, spelling (and sometimes punctuation) is silently modernised.

Introduction

I

The word 'utopia' entered the world with the publication of More's little book in December 1516. More coined it by fusing the Greek adverb *ou* – 'not' – with the noun *topos* – 'place' – and giving the resulting compound a Latin ending. Within the book's fiction, 'Noplace' is a newly discovered island somewhere in the New World. The meaning that 'utopia' has come to have as a common noun – a perfect society, or a literary account of one – seems authorised by the full title of the book, which is (translating from the Latin), 'Concerning the Best State of a Commonwealth and the New Island of Utopia'. The same Hellenist readers who recognised the etymology of 'Utopia' would also find this meaning suggested by the fact that the word puns on another Greek compound, *eutopia* – 'happy' or 'fortunate' place.

When we begin to read the book itself, though, the plausible supposition that *Utopia* is a utopia is rapidly undermined. First, the explorer whose account of the new island the book purports to record turns out to be named 'Hythloday' – another Greek compound, signifying 'expert in nonsense'. Second, the introductory, scene-setting pages are followed not by an account of Utopia but by a lengthy debate on the question whether it is worthwhile for Hythloday to enter practical politics by joining a king's council. Within this debate is another, recounted by Hythloday, on the problem of theft in More's England. Apart from a comic postlude to the second one, these two debates seem deadly serious, and they are powerfully written: but what are they doing in a book on the ideal commonwealth? And when, at the beginning of the second part (or 'Book') of *Utopia*, we at last reach Hythloday's account of the new island, it is still not clear that we've reached eutopia.

The commonwealth of Utopia turns out to be a highly attractive place in some ways, but a highly unattractive one in others. No one goes hungry there, no one is homeless. The commonwealth is strikingly egalitarian. On the other hand, personal freedom is restricted in ways large and small. Discussing political issues outside the senate or the popular assembly is a capital offence; a citizen must get permission from the local magistrates to travel, and from spouse and father even to go for a walk in the country. In general, if Utopia anticipates the welfare democracies of our own time in many respects, the elaborate constraints imposed on its citizens also frequently put us in mind of modern totalitarian regimes. More's own society was rigidly hierarchical and highly regulated, so Utopia may not have seemed as restrictive to him as it does to us. Still, it is difficult to believe that he would have regarded as ideal all the features of Utopia that we find unattractive. Moreover, every Utopian proper noun embodies the same kind of learned joke as 'Utopia' and 'Hythloday'; and a few, at least, of the Utopian exploits and customs we are told about are hard to take seriously. Finally, at the end of the book More partly dissociates himself – or at least the dramatic character who goes by his name – from Utopia, saying that many of its laws and customs struck him as absurd, though there are many others that he would 'like rather than expect' to see in Europe.

These observations suggest three fundamental questions about *Utopia*. First, why did More invent a flawed commonwealth? It is easy to understand why a writer would want to create a fictional account of an ideal commonwealth, or a satire of a bad one. But what's the point of inventing a commonwealth that is partly good and partly bad? Second, what do the debates of Book I have to do with the account of Utopia in Book II, and with the subject of the best condition of the commonwealth? Third, how are we to understand the fact that More represents himself as disapproving of much of what Hythloday says – and that, by peppering the book with jokes, he even seems to deny its seriousness?

Utopia is endlessly enigmatic, and we don't pretend to have definitive answers to these questions, or to many others that the book prompts. But we can provide the necessary starting point for interpretation, and offer some tentative answers to our questions, by setting *Utopia* in the context of More's life and times, and the history of political thought. In this process, the introduction provides the broad outlines, and the annotations to the text fill in details.

II

More was born in London on 7 February 1478, or possibly 1477.[1] His father, John More, was determined that his eldest son should follow him into the legal profession. Thomas spent a few years at St Anthony's School, learning the fundamentals of Latin grammar and composition. At the age of about twelve, he was placed as a page in the household of Henry VII's Lord Chancellor, John Morton. (Morton was also Archbishop of Canterbury and, from 1493, a cardinal.) This placement was ideally suited to exposing More to the ways of public life, and to securing him a powerful patron. After two years at Morton's, the boy was sent to Oxford, presumably to sharpen the skills in rhetoric and logic that would be important to a legal career. He was then, at about sixteen, brought back to London to begin legal training in the Inns of Court.

During his years as a law student, however, More came increasingly under the influence of a group of literary scholars, central figures of the emerging tradition of Renaissance humanism in England. In the Renaissance, 'humanism' meant not so much a philosophical position as a particular scholarly orientation. The term 'humanist' derives from *studia humanitatis*, a Ciceronian phrase that came to designate a family of disciplines: grammar, rhetoric, history, poetry and moral philosophy.[2] As in the Middle Ages, Latin remained the normal language of learning. Beginning in the fourteenth century, humanists like Petrarch attempted to revive the classical form of that language; by the early fifteenth century, they had undertaken a parallel attempt for classical Greek. More studied Latin composition with the grammarian John Holt, and Greek under William Grocyn. He also fell strongly under the influence of John Colet. Like Grocyn, Colet had studied in Italy, the centre of humanist learning. After his return to England in 1496, he gave

---

[1] See the most recent biography: Richard Marius, *Thomas More*, p. 7.
[2] See Paul Oskar Kristeller, *Renaissance Thought: The Classic, Scholastic, and Humanist Strains* (New York, 1961), pp. 8–23.

several series of lectures at Oxford on the epistles of St Paul, lectures that constituted the earliest English application of some of the exegetical and historiographical techniques of Italian humanism; later he became Dean of St Paul's Cathedral, and founded there the first of the humanist grammar schools in England. And in 1499, More made the acquaintance of the great Dutch humanist Erasmus, who in that year first visited England.

Indeed, at this period More seems to have been at least as intent on the pursuit of literary scholarship as of the law. He also seriously considered becoming a priest – doubtless in part because scholarship was almost exclusively the province of clerics. According to a biographical sketch of More that Erasmus wrote in 1519, for a time 'he applied his whole mind to the pursuit of piety, with vigils and fasts and prayer and similar exercises preparing himself for the priesthood' (*CWE*, VII, 21). In fact More seems to have tested his vocation not merely for the priesthood – a calling that, as Morton's example shows, need not have precluded a legal career – but also for a life of religious withdrawal. The biography by his son-in-law William Roper says that at about this time More lived for four years with the Carthusians, the strictest of the monastic orders.[3]

Eventually More made his choices. In late 1504 or early 1505, he closed the door to the priesthood and monasticism by marrying Jane Colt; nor is there any sign, in the period following his marriage, that he thought of abandoning the law. Given the necessity of supporting a growing family – Jane bore him four children before her death in 1511, after which More married a middle-aged widow, Alice Middleton – he could scarcely afford to entertain such thoughts.

In the decade following his first marriage, More rose rapidly in the legal profession. Roper says that he was a member of the Parliament of 1504, and he almost certainly represented the City of London in that of 1510. In the same year, he began to act as a city judge, having been appointed an Undersheriff of London. Increasingly he won assignments that drew on his literary and rhetorical as well as his legal skills. By August 1517, and perhaps somewhat earlier, he had entered Henry VIII's council.[4] His first conciliar assignment was as a diplomat, in a trade mission to Calais. And though his subsequent

[3] *The Life of Sir Thomas More*, p. 198.
[4] J. A. Guy, *The Public Career of Sir Thomas More*, pp. 6–7.

assignments spanned a broad range of activities, his main employment, before he became Lord Chancellor in 1529, was as secretary to the king. He also served frequently as the king's orator. And when Henry decided to write against Martin Luther (in 1520), More acted as his literary adviser and editor.

In the earlier part of his professional life, More also managed to carry out a substantial amount of independent scholarship and writing. It is striking how precisely his works of this period conform to the five associated disciplines of the *studia humanitatis*.[5] As grammarian (in the Renaissance understanding of the term), he translated Greek poems, and four short works by the Greek ironist Lucian. As rhetorician, he wrote a declamation in reply to Lucian's *Tyrannicide*. (The declamation was a standard rhetorical exercise, a speech on a paradoxical or otherwise ingenious topic, often involving the impersonation of some historical or mythical figure.) Erasmus reports a lost dialogue, evidently in the spirit of a declamation, defending the community of wives advocated in Plato's *Republic*. Several of More's longer, polemical letters of these years belong to the rhetorical genre of the invective. As poet, he wrote, in addition to a few English poems, a large number of Latin epigrams. As historian, he practised the humanist genre of historical biography, in Latin and English versions of his unfinished *History of King Richard III* (a splendid, sardonic work that became the main source of Shakespeare's play), and in his translation of a biography of the fifteenth-century Italian philosopher Pico della Mirandola. As moral and political philosopher, he wrote *Utopia*. The publication of *Utopia* came near the end of this phase of More's literary career. For several years after 1516, he wrote little, other than what was required of him in his profession; and when he resumed writing books in the 1520s – works opposing the Lutheran 'heresy', and a series of devotional works – they no longer fitted the humanist categories.

---

[5] See P. O. Kristeller, 'Thomas More as a Renaissance Humanist', *Moreana*, no. 65–6 (1980), 5–22.

III

Utopia was conceived in the summer of 1515. In May of that year, More left England for Flanders, as a member of a royal trade commission. The negotiations of this commission with its Flemish counterpart at Bruges were stalled and recessed by 21 July, but More did not return to England until 25 October. In the three months from late July to late October, he enjoyed a rare period of leisure; it was during this period that *Utopia* began to take shape.

At some point in the summer More visited Antwerp, where he met Peter Giles, to whom Erasmus had recommended him. Giles was a man after More's own heart. He was a classical scholar, and an intimate of Erasmus and his circle; he was also a man of practical affairs, city clerk of Antwerp and as such deeply involved in the business of that cosmopolitan shipping and commercial centre. Book I of *Utopia* opens with a brief account of the trade mission, which leads into an account of More's acquaintance with Giles. At this point, the book glides from fact into fiction. More says he encountered Giles after Mass one day, and Giles introduced him to Raphael Hythloday, with whom they proceeded to have the conversation that is recorded in *Utopia*. This fictional conversation is presumably the transformation and expansion of actual conversations between More and Giles.[6]

We have no direct information as to when More began writing the book. In his biographical sketch, Erasmus reported that More wrote the second book of *Utopia* 'earlier, when at leisure; at a later opportunity he added the first in the heat of the moment' (*CWE*, VII, 24). As J. H. Hexter argues, if More wrote Book II first, it seems very likely that he initially regarded it as a complete work; presumably this version of *Utopia* was well in hand by the time he returned to England.[7] Back in London, though, he found reason to add the dialogue of Book I.

Hexter points out that the first version of *Utopia* must have included not only the account of Utopia that now occupies all but the last few pages of Book II but also an introduction something like the opening of the present Book I. Otherwise it would not be clear who is

---

[6] Giles seems to hint as much in the commendatory letter he wrote for the first edition of *Utopia:* see p. 124.

[7] See *More's 'Utopia': The Biography of an Idea*, pp. 15–30; *CW*, IV (*Utopia*), xv–xxiii.

speaking in the monologue on Utopia, and under what circumstances. The second phase of composition must have begun, not with the embassy to Bruges and the diversion to Antwerp, but with the dialogue of Book I. Indeed the precise point where More, as Hexter says, 'opened a seam' in the first version of *Utopia* to insert the dialogue can be identified with some confidence (see below, p. 12n). After writing the dialogue, More must also have revised the conclusion of the work as a whole. In the final paragraph of Book II, as Hexter points out, the narrator recalls what Hythloday 'had said about certain counsellors who were afraid they might not appear knowing enough unless they found something to criticise in other men's ideas'. But Hythloday's censures occur in the dialogue of Book I (p. 14), so that this allusion to them must have been written after the dialogue.

The fact that *Utopia* was composed in this odd sequence presumably has implications for its interpretation. As with many other facts about the book, though, this one cuts two ways. On the one hand, it may suggest that More split open a complete, unified book to insert a dialogue which, though interesting in itself, doesn't really belong with the original material – that *Utopia* is really *two* books. Or it may suggest that More had second thoughts about the account of Utopia and saw a need to insert a new section which would be in effect an introduction to it. In any event, the dialogue affects our view of Utopia. For one thing, it gives us a much sharper sense of Hythloday, who is both our only source of information about the island commonwealth and its foremost enthusiast.

IV

More's book benefited greatly both from his experience in law and politics and from his humanist learning. Though the social problems *Utopia* addresses are perennial, the particular formulations of them, and the data of recent and contemporary English and European life that the book deploys, reflect More's personal and professional experience. But the intellectual paradigms that he brings to bear on the understanding of these problems, and the form and style of his book, derive primarily from his literary humanism.

The most obvious relation between *Utopia* and More's humanist learning is that with the central Greek works of political philosophy.

More's title identifies the book as belonging to the oldest genre of political writing, the discourse on the ideal commonwealth initiated by Plato's *Republic* and *Laws* and continued in Aristotle's *Politics* – and subsequently in many other works. Plato's and Aristotle's discussions of the ideal commonwealth are, however, purely argumentative, whereas the Utopian part of More's book consists of Hythloday's fictional travelogue. The decision to present his imaginary society in the form of a long speech by a fictional personage is responsible both for much of the book's interest and for much of its enigmatic quality. Fictions are attractive, but they tend not to resolve into unambiguous meanings.[8]

For the debate of Book I, the obvious formal models are the dialogues of Plato – or those of Cicero, which, like *Utopia* and unlike the Platonic dialogues, consist of long speeches punctuated by brief interruptions. There are also precedents for the main *topic* of the debate, in humanist as well as classical literature. Arguing about whether Hythloday should join a king's council is a way of getting at the general, and very frequently discussed, problem of 'counsel': the problem of ensuring that rulers receive and take appropriate advice. As Quentin Skinner observes, this problem could be approached either from the point of view of the ruler, in which case the focus is on 'the importance of choosing good councillors and learning to distinguish between true and false friends', or from the point of view of the prospective councillor, when the focus is on the question whether it is wise for a scholar to commit himself to practical politics.[9] Viewed in the second perspective, it is an aspect of the ancient question of the relative merits of the active and contemplative lives.[10] Since, as Skinner says, 'humanists tended to see themselves essentially as political advisers', counsel was the political

---

[8] More's decision to present Utopia as a fiction has also been responsible for much of his book's influence: the literary genre of the utopia, which *Utopia* initiated, differs from the philosophical discourse on the ideal commonwealth precisely in that it offers a fictionalised account of the eutopia as if it already existed. In the second of the two letters on *Utopia* that More addressed to Giles, he commented obliquely on the advantage of this way of proceeding. See p. 113.

[9] *The Foundations of Modern Political Thought*, I, 216–17.

[10] Influential and interesting treatments of the issue are found in Plato (*Republic* VI.496C–497B and Epistle VII) and Seneca ('On Leisure' and 'On Tranquillity of Mind', in *Moral Essays*), who make the case for non-involvement, and in one of Plutarch's *Moral Essays*, 'That a Philosopher Ought to Converse Especially with Men in Power'. Cicero sees merit in both courses (*On Moral Obligation* I.xx.69–xxi.72, xliii.153–xliv.156).

topic that most intrigued them. More himself had special reason to be intrigued: he had been moving closer to full-time royal service, and, in the period when he wrote the dialogue of Book I, he seems to have been pondering a first invitation to join Henry's council.[11] This would be a professional move towards which all his training and experience as lawyer and diplomat pointed, and yet contemplating it would have prompted some anxiety in a man who was also imbued with the ideals of scholarly and religious detachment.

Though the topic of counsel is commonplace, More's treatment of it is distinctive. This is also the case with his treatment (in the dialogue-within-a-dialogue) of the problem of theft, which expands into a general analysis of the condition of England. More's handling of these matters differs from that of most other social or political writers of the period in what we may call its systemic or holistic approach. As Hexter puts it, More sees 'in depth, in perspective, and in mutual relation problems which his contemporaries saw in the flat and as a disjointed series' (*CW*, IV, ci). He understands that the problem of counsel cannot be solved by sending a few wise men to court, because, in the existing structure of society, most of the people they would encounter there – including especially the rulers – are motivated by blinkered self-interest. Similarly, the problem of theft cannot be solved by punishing thieves, because theft stems primarily from poverty, which is in turn the product of a number of social factors. The polity as a whole is a complex network of reciprocally affecting parts.

The social analysis of Book I is also distinguished by its passionate intensity, its pervasive moral outrage at the status quo. The analysis of the problem of theft constitutes a scathing indictment of a system of 'justice' in which the poor are 'driven to the awful necessity of stealing and then dying for it' (p. 16). The root cause of this situation lies in the pride, sloth and greed of the upper classes. Noblemen live idly off others' labour, and also 'drag around with them a great train of idle servants', who, when they are later dismissed, know no honest way of making a living. The practice of enclosure (fencing common land as pasturage for sheep) deprives farm labourers of their livelihood and sets them to wander and beg – or to steal and be hanged.

[11] See Jerry Mermel, 'Preparations for a Politic Life: Sir Thomas More's Entry into the King's Service', *The Journal of Medieval and Renaissance Studies*, 7 (1977), 53–66.

Though it is Hythloday who delivers this indictment, one can hardly doubt that it embodies More's own views; and in fact More represents himself as concurring in Hythloday's analysis (p. 28). In the debate on counsel, however, Hythloday and More take opposite positions, with Hythloday opposing involvement and More favouring it. Both positions are powerfully argued, and they are never bridged: at the end of Book I, the disputants simply drop the topic and go on to another – the desirability of abolishing private property – about which they also never reach agreement.

These facts suggest another aspect of the relation between *Utopia* and its author's character and experience, one that helps to explain More's apparent dissociation of himself from Utopia: that the personality and views of his two main characters project his own persistent dividedness of mind. That 'More' closely resembles the author is clear. Yet it is equally clear that this cautious, practical lawyer and family man is More without his passion and vision – a More who could not have written *Utopia*, nor ever have chosen martyrdom. The most obvious models for Hythloday are the stern experts on comparative politics of Plato's political dialogues. In the book's generic economy, Hythloday corresponds to the austere Stranger of the *Statesman* or the Old Athenian of the *Laws*, whose detachment from practical affairs enables them to see and speak the truth. But this is as much as to say that Hythloday is to some extent More's fantasy – partly wistful, partly critical – of what he himself might have been, had he made different choices a decade earlier; even as 'More' is his slightly deprecating representation of the practical man he had become.

More's dividedness of mind is also related, via his humanist learning, to the seriocomic mode of *Utopia.* Here the key author is Lucian, four of whose works, as we noted above, More had translated. (These were published in 1506, together with some additional translations by Erasmus.)

Lucian was a Syrian sophist of the second century AD, one of the last writers of classical Greek. In a series of dialogues and other short prose pieces, he played a key part in the development of a tradition of making serious points under the guise of jokes, other examples of which are the *Golden Ass* of Apuleius, numerous mock orations and festive treatises (like those listed as precedents in Erasmus' preface to *The Praise of Folly*), and works of later writers like

Rabelais and Swift. This tradition is sometimes characterised by the Latin phrase *serio ludere* – 'to play seriously'.[12]

As More says in his preface to the translations of Lucian, this kind of writing satisfies the Horatian injunction that literature should combine delight with instruction (*CW*, III, Part 1, 3); in his second letter to Giles, he indicates that this was why he chose a seriocomic mode for *Utopia*. But More was also attracted to the tradition of *serio ludere* for another, deeper reason. The divided, complex mind – capable of seeing more than one side of a question and reluctant to make a definite commitment to any single position – has a proclivity for ironic discourse; and *serio ludere* – in which the play can serve to qualify or undercut any statement – is one of the great vehicles of irony. The first major humanist work in the Lucianic tradition is *The Praise of Folly* (1509). This is a declamation of bewilderingly complex irony, in which Erasmus has Folly (supposed to be a goddess) praise folly – thus setting up a sort of verbal hall of mirrors. The situation in *Utopia* is equally complex: an 'expert in nonsense' condemns Europe and praises Noplace; and his views – many of which are clearly not nonsense – are reported by a character who bears the author's name, and who does not always approve of them.

V

Turning now to the question of the relation between the two books of *Utopia*, it is evident, first, that an analysis of the evils of existing society forms an appropriate prelude to a discussion of a possibly better one; and that the juxtaposition of Europe and Utopia throws sharply into relief what is distinctive about each. The resulting comparisons are the burden of the peroration of Book II, in which Hythloday eloquently sums up what we've seen about Europe and Utopia, and makes, very powerfully, the contrasts that are begging to be made. But Book I also prepares us for Book II in another way, which becomes apparent if we consider the structure of Hythloday's arguments in Book I.

The discussion of theft opens with the question why this problem continues unabated despite the execution of so many thieves.

[12] See, for example, Edgar Wind, *Pagan Mysteries in the Renaissance*, rev. edn (New York, 1968), esp. pp. 236–7, and Rosalie L. Colie, *Paradoxia Epidemica: The Renaissance Tradition of Paradox* (Princeton, 1966).

Hythloday's response begins with, and is organised by, the contention that executing thieves is neither moral nor practical: 'The penalty is too harsh in itself, yet it isn't an effective deterrent. Simple theft is not so great a crime that it ought to cost a man his head, yet no punishment however severe can restrain men from robbery when they have no other way to eat' (p. 16). Correspondingly, Hythloday argues that the milder punishment he recommends is both just and expedient.

As More's contemporaries would have recognised, this strategy of argument originates in rhetorical theory. Rhetoric (like logic) provided lists of subject-matter headings, called 'topics', of proven utility in constructing arguments. Since the subject of Hythloday's remarks is the advisability or inadvisability of particular policies, his speeches belong to the 'deliberative' genre, the oratory of persuasion and dissuasion. The central topics of deliberative oratory are *honestas* and *utilitas* – honour and expediency.[13] The deliberative orator normally argues that a particular course of action is advisable on the ground that it is honourable, or on the ground that it is expedient – or argues that it is *in*advisable, as being either dishonourable or inexpedient. Naturally, the strongest case is made when it can be shown that considerations of honour and expediency point in the same direction.

This turns out to be the nature of Hythloday's argument not only on the problem of theft but on all the questions he addresses. To 'More' and Giles he argues that joining a king's council would be neither honourable nor useful, since kings use councillors only to tell them how best to accomplish dishonourable and destructive ends. In the two narratives of imaginary privy council meetings that he uses as examples, he portrays himself as arguing that the supposedly expedient courses recommended by the other councillors are both immoral and self-defeating. When 'More', at the climax of the debate on counsel, argues for an 'indirect', temporising approach, in which the councillor, knowing that he cannot turn all to good, will at least try to make things as little bad as possible, Hythloday responds that such a strategy is neither practical nor consistent with Christian morality. Indeed, we get the strong impression

---

[13] See, for example, Cicero, *On Invention* II.li.156–8; Quintilian, *The Education of the Orator* III.viii.1–3, 22–5.

that he would say that the moral and the expedient *never* truly conflict, that correct analysis will always show that a dishonourable
course is also impractical. This position links him with the Stoics,
for whom (as Cicero explains in *Of Moral Obligation*) the identity of
the moral and the expedient is a key doctrine.

Evidently the question of the relation of the moral and the expedient interested More deeply, as it did other humanists. The claim
that the two are identical was a standard theme of early humanist
political thought, which is permeated by Stoicism; but in the fifteenth century, some Italian humanists began to assert that *honestas* is
not always the same as *utilitas*. In 1513, Machiavelli produced, in *The
Prince*, the most famous of all statements of this position. More could
not have known Machiavelli's book (it wasn't published until 1532),
but he certainly knew the tradition of thought that it crystallised.

The question was not merely timely, though, or merely relevant to
the topics of practical politics debated in Book I. It is also linked with
the subject of the best condition of the commonwealth. If the moral
and the expedient are ultimately identical, then it is theoretically
possible to design a commonwealth that would always act morally.
But if the moral and the expedient cannot be fully reconciled, then
this ideal could never be achieved, even in theory.

That More recognised the importance of this issue to the theory
of the ideal commonwealth seems clear from what follows the
exchange about the indirect approach to counsel. The question of
the validity of this approach is never resolved – surely because More
was of two minds about it. In the fiction, though, the question is left
unresolved because it is sidetracked by Hythloday's sudden confession that he thinks the abolition of private property offers the only
route to social justice. 'More' disputes the claim, not on the ground
that communism is unjust, but on the basis of arguments (derived
from Aristotle's critique of the *Republic*) that it is impractical. The
commonwealth cannot be stable, prosperous and happy without private property and the inequality that goes with it. Hythloday coun-
ters that More would think differently if he had seen Utopia: for that
commonwealth embodies the equality that More thinks impractical,
and yet it is uniquely happy and well-governed, with institutions
that are both 'wise and sacred' (p. 38).

This, then, is the context that More provided for the account of
Utopia: a dispute about the degree of compatibility of the moral and

the expedient in political life, and in particular about whether the ideal of equality is compatible with stability and prosperity. This context suggests that the account of Utopia is – whatever else it may also be – an attempt to answer this fundamental question about the best condition of the commonwealth. Is it possible, even theoretically, for a commonwealth to be both moral and expedient?[14]

VI

To construct Utopia, More applied the method for designing an ideal commonwealth devised by Plato and Aristotle. In this method, creating such a commonwealth is not simply a matter of piling together all the desirable features one can think of. On the contrary, the design premise is the principle of *autarkeia*, self-sufficiency: the best commonwealth will be one that includes everything that is *necessary* to the happiness of its citizens, and nothing else.

Starting from this economical premise, Plato developed, and Aristotle refined, a four-step procedure for constructing an ideal commonwealth.[15] First, one must determine what constitutes the happiest life for the individual. This is the central question of ethical theory, and, as Aristotle explains at the beginning of Book VII of the *Politics*, its answer constitutes the starting point of political theory. Second, from these conclusions about the most desirable life, the theorist derives the communal goals whose attainment will result in the happiness of the citizens. Third, it is necessary to form a sort of checklist of the physical and institutional components that the commonwealth must include: a certain amount of population will be required, and a certain kind and extent of territory; certain occupational functions will have to be performed; and so on. Finally, the theorist determines the particular form that each of

---

[14] These considerations suggest a solution to the much-discussed problem of why More made Utopia non-Christian. More and all his contemporaries – including Machiavelli – believed that moral, and Christian, behaviour is advisable on religious grounds. One of the liveliest questions in early sixteenth-century political thought, though, is that raised in Book I of *Utopia*: how far, in political life, is this kind of behaviour advisable on purely prudential grounds? More realised that this question could be answered by seeing what a society pursuing perfect expediency through purely rational calculations would be like.

[15] See Plato, *Republic* II.369B–372E; Aristotle, *Politics* VII.i–viii.

these components should be given in order to assure that, collectively, they will constitute the best commonwealth.

It seems clear that Book II of *Utopia* presents the results of a best-commonwealth exercise performed according to the Greek rules – though More's decision to present his results in the form of an account of a supposedly existing commonwealth entailed suppressing or disguising the various components of the dialectical substructure of his model. But once we recognise that Book II of *Utopia* constitutes a best-commonwealth exercise, some mystifying aspects of the work begin to make sense. In particular, this recognition tells us how to take the lengthy account of Utopian moral philosophy (pp. 66–77); and it can suggest an answer to the key question we posed in starting out: why did More portray a flawed commonwealth?

The passage on moral philosophy is in fact the cornerstone of the Utopian edifice. It constitutes the first step of the best-commonwealth exercise, the determination of the happiest life for the individual. The Utopians (who take it for granted that self-interest is the basic fact of human nature) maintain that pleasure is the goal of life, but they find that the most pleasurable life is the life of virtue. This is also the conclusion of Plato and Aristotle, but for them the virtuous life is that of contemplative leisure, made possible by the labour of slaves and artisans whose happiness is not a goal of the commonwealth. By contrast, the Utopians conclude that individual felicity is incompatible with special privilege, and think that the foremost pleasures 'arise from practice of the virtues and consciousness of a good life' (p. 75). Thus, though the Utopians are not Christians and their arguments consider only self-interest, they conclude that the best life for the individual is one lived in accordance with the moral norms of Christian culture. Moreover, parallels between their arguments and passages in others of More's works confirm that he thought these arguments valid – though most readers find them convoluted and strained.

But even if we grant that for each individual morality is always expedient, is this also true for the commonwealth as a whole? For the most part, Utopia supports this view. If, as the Utopians conclude, one's happiness is incompatible with spoiling the happiness of others, then it follows that the institutions of the commonwealth, whose goal is to maximise the happiness of its citizens, must be structured so as to implement the Golden Rule. Indeed, the institutions and policies of Utopia – many of which derive from previous treatments of the ideal commonwealth – are on the whole far preferable to those of European nations, and are in many respects completely consistent with Christian standards, as those are interpreted in the writings of More and his associates.

Yet some Utopian practices are incompatible with these standards, and would seem to be justifiable only on grounds of expediency. To take the most disturbing examples, there is, first, the severe restriction of personal freedom. In Book I, Hythloday criticises repressive policies on the ground that 'it's an incompetent monarch who can reform his people only by depriving them of all life's pleasures' (p. 34), and this attitude harmonises with many passages in the writings of More's humanist circle. The Utopians themselves believe that 'no kind of pleasure is forbidden, provided harm does not come of it' (p. 60). But in fact, as we pointed out earlier, their lives are hedged round with an extraordinary number and range of prohibitions: freedom of political speech is severely restricted, as is freedom of movement; even the use of leisure time is limited to a few approved activities.

Then there are the troubling aspects of Utopian foreign policy. For the most part, the Utopians are generous towards their neighbours. They distribute their surplus commodities among them 'at moderate prices', and they are always happy to provide them with skilful and honest administrators (pp. 61, 85). They detest war, and, whenever it cannot be avoided, go to great lengths to minimise its destructiveness. Yet it turns out that they will go to war for a good many reasons – including to obtain territory for colonisation, whenever the Utopian population exceeds the optimum number. Furthermore, some of their military tactics are of very dubious morality. They offer rewards for the assassination of enemy leaders. They employ mercenaries to do as much of their fighting as possible; and the mercenaries they prefer are the savage Zapoletes, whose use is hard to reconcile with the aim of minimising war's destructiveness. And, despite their compassion for the common citizens of enemy nations, the Utopians enslave the prisoners taken in wars in which they have employed their own forces.[16]

[16] Robert P. Adams shows that many of the 'antichivalric' Utopian military practices are consonant with Stoic and Erasmian humanist ideas (*The Better Part of Valor*, pp. 152–4). But this argument cannot explain the particular practices mentioned here.

The explanation of these discrepancies between Utopian practices and More's own ideals would seem to lie in his recognition of the fact that even in the best commonwealth there will always be conflicts between valid goals – a problem that seems rarely to occur to theorists of the ideal commonwealth or writers of utopias. More's awareness of the conflict of goals is first apparent in the section on moral philosophy. Utopian ethics is a strange fusion of Stoicism and Epicureanism. One feature of Epicureanism that seems to interest More greatly is the so-called 'hedonic calculus', Epicurus' rule that, in choosing among pleasures, one should always choose a greater pleasure over a lesser, and should reject any pleasure that will eventually result in pain: this formula occurs three times in one form or another in the passage on moral philosophy. It seems clear that More thinks that similar principles should be applied to resolving conflicts between goals at the political level; and it is in terms of such principles that we should understand most of the unattractive features of Utopia.

More was evidently impressed by the Aristotelian objections to egalitarianism that he puts into his own mouth at the end of Book i. If Utopia does not suffer from the chaos that 'More' had claimed would be inevitable in a communist society, this is presumably because of the elaborate system of constraints that More has built into it. Apparently he believed that too much freedom would threaten the stability and security of the commonwealth – which, in the nature of things, has to be the political goal of highest priority. The rulers of some modern states have struck a similar balance.

The same line of explanation applies to the distressing Utopian practices in foreign policy. It is impossible to believe that More approved of all these practices; yet evidently he thought them necessary. The internal arrangements of Utopia or any other commonwealth won't really matter unless the commonwealth can be made externally secure; and as long as other commonwealths are not utopian, it is hard to see how to secure it without indulging in some practices that are expedient but certainly not moral.

Despite its abundant wit, *Utopia* is in fact a pretty melancholy book. More shared with St Augustine (whose *City of God* he had expounded in a series of lectures in about 1501) the conviction that no human society could be wholly attractive; and even the attractive arrangements that are theoretically possible are in practice very difficult to achieve. There is no reason not to take at face value the final judgement of 'More' that Utopia includes 'many features that in our own societies I would like rather than expect to see'. Yet 'More' also insists, in the debate on the 'indirect approach' to counsel, that things can be made at least a little less bad, by working tactfully on kings and councillors. Indeed, many of the reforms proposed in *Utopia* have been effected in the centuries since it was written – though not always by peaceful means, and not always resulting in clear net improvements.

Note on the translation

A translation of *Utopia* has to be based on one of the first four editions – the only ones in which More or his direct agents had a hand. (There is no manuscript of the work.) These editions were published at Louvain (1516), Paris (1517) and Basel (March and November 1518). Like other recent editors, we have concluded that the Basel editions most nearly and fully represent More's intent, both for his text itself and for its appendages (contributions by other humanists) and format. The second of these Basel editions is a close resetting of the first, with nothing, in our judgement, to suggest that its changes from the earlier version have authorial sanction. We have therefore based the translation on the edition of March 1518, occasionally corrected by better readings in the other three early editions, and here and there emended by editorial judgement – our own or that of our predecessors.

Utopia is not cast in artificial or ornate literary language, as More's age understood it. Though More occasionally uses rare words, on the whole his Latin is simple, conversational, everyday prose such as a lawyer, a diplomat or a humanist scholar might employ about the normal occasions and business of daily existence. It is far from Ciceronian; it is seldom deliberately mannered. But it is quite unlike modern English in several important ways. The sentences are longer and less tightly knit in patterns of subordination. The main idea of a sentence may be hidden in an ablative absolute, or hung out at a considerable distance in space and syntax. Because it is a highly inflected language, Latin can scatter the ingredients of a sentence about more loosely than English does, in the assurance that a reader will be able to assemble them within his or her own mind. An English sentence is expected to do more of the reader's work. At the same time, Latin, or at least More's lawyerly Latin, has a mass of delicate innuendoes and qualifications at its disposal – double negatives, ironic appositives, pseudo-antitheses and formal (but only formal) correlatives. To represent the structure of More's Latin syntax in English would create the impression of a whirling chaos; reproducing his stylistic nuances would give rise to a mincing and artificial English. And in either case, the real flavour of More's book, which is casual and colloquial, would be lost.

The almost inevitable solution is to translate into natural, unmannered, everyday prose, and let the flowers of rhetoric wither by the wayside. With some texts this procedure might produce a flat or neutral version; but *Utopia* is not only free and various in itself, it is so crowded with thought that shoehorning More's overflowing amplitude of meaning into pronounceable English sentences provides work enough for a translator. The complexities of interpreting *Utopia* don't, on the whole, derive from intricacies of language; they are matters of attitude and levels of ironic reversal – both controlled by the sort of moral feeling one brings to the book.

Finally, a word about the appendages to the text. More entrusted the publication of *Utopia* to Giles and Erasmus. One or both of them composed a series of marginal glosses on the text (see p. 125 and note), and, in accordance with More's wish, Erasmus secured a series of commendatory letters, poems and other materials to buttress the work (see p. 114n). These commendations appeared in different combinations in all four early editions, some preceding the text of *Utopia* itself, and others following it. Since the commendations – and, we assume, the glosses – were appended to the text with More's approval, and since all these materials are useful in indicating how *Utopia* struck the readers for whom it was originally intended, we have included them in this edition. We have, though, relegated all the commendations to the end of the text.

Chronology

1478 (1477?) 7 February: More's birth.

1485 Defeat and death of Richard III at Bosworth Field; accession of Henry VII.

c. 1490–2 More serves as page in Cardinal Morton's household.

c. 1492–4 More at Oxford.

c. 1494 More enters the Inns of Court to study law.

1499 More meets Erasmus.

1504 More in Parliament?

1504 or 1505 More marries Jane Colt.

c. 1504–7 Publication of accounts of the New World voyages of Amerigo Vespucci.

1509 Death of Henry VII; accession of Henry VIII. Erasmus writes *The Praise of Folly* (published 1511).

1510 More appointed Undersheriff of London.

1511 Death of Jane Colt; More marries Alice Middleton.

1512–13 Henry VIII at war with France.

1513 Machiavelli writes *The Prince* (published 1532).

c. 1513–18 More writes *The History of King Richard the Third*.

1515 May–October: More on embassy to Flanders; meets Peter Giles; begins *Utopia*.

1516 December: *Utopia* published at Louvain.

1517 More joins Henry VIII's council. Second edition of *Utopia* published at Paris. Martin Luther's ninety-five theses on indulgences signal the beginning of the Reformation.

1518 March and November: third and fourth editions of *Utopia* published at Basel, together with *Epigrams*. (These are the last editions of *Utopia* in which More could have had a hand.)

1521 More becomes Under-Treasurer of the Exchequer; knighted.
His daughter Margaret marries William Roper.

1523 More Speaker of the House of Commons. Writes a defence of
Henry VIII against Luther.

1525 More appointed Chancellor of the Duchy of Lancaster.

1529 More publishes *A Dialogue Concerning Heresies* against Luther
and Tyndale. 25 October: appointed Lord Chancellor of England (first layman to occupy that office).

1532 16 May: More resigns the Chancellorship over the 'Sub-
mission of the Clergy', which ceded veto power over ecclesiastical legislation to Henry VIII.

1533 Henry VIII marries Anne Boleyn and is excommunicated.

1534 13 April: More refuses to swear support for the Act of Suc-
cession (acknowledging Henry's children by Anne Boleyn as
heirs to the throne). 17 April: More imprisoned in the Tower of
London, where he writes *A Dialogue of Comfort against Tribulation* and other devotional works.

1535 1 July: More tried and convicted of treason. 6 July: beheaded.

1551 *Utopia* first translated into English, by Ralph Robinson.

1557 Collected edition of More's English works.

1565–6 Collected edition of More's Latin works.

1935 More canonised.

Suggestions for further reading

The earliest biography of More is the ingenuous and engaging *Life of Sir Thomas More* by his son-in-law William Roper. It is published with the other famous English biography of the early sixteenth century, George Cavendish's *The Life and Death of Cardinal Wolsey*, in *Two Early Tudor Lives*, ed. Richard S. Sylvester and Davis P. Harding (New Haven and London, 1962). By far the most influential modern biography is R. W. Chambers' *Thomas More* (London, 1935). The most recent is Richard Marius, *Thomas More* (New York, 1984), which offers a resolutely unflattering portrait of More in sharp contrast to its predecessors'. More's professional life is traced by J. A. Guy, *The Public Career of Sir Thomas More* (New Haven and London, 1980). Alistair Fox interprets More's works in the context of an exploration of his complex psychology in *Thomas More: History and Providence* (New Haven and London, 1983). A rich and convenient source of biographical information about More's contemporaries is *Contemporaries of Erasmus: A Biographical Register of the Renaissance and Reformation*, ed. Peter G. Bietenholz and Thomas B. Deutscher, 3 vols. (Toronto/Buffalo/London, 1985–7).

The most authoritative editions of More's works are those of the fifteen-volume Yale edition of the *Complete Works of St Thomas More*, now nearly complete. A Modernized Series supplement to the Yale edition provides translations of forty-four of More's Latin letters and texts of twenty-two English ones: *Selected Letters*, ed. Elizabeth F. Rogers (rev. edn, 1967). *Utopia* (Latin and English), ed. Edward Surtz, SJ, and J. H. Hexter (1965), is Volume IV of the Yale edition. Hexter's section of the introduction to that volume constitutes the single most challenging and interesting interpretation of *Utopia*; Surtz's section, and his 300-page commentary, supply a wealth of information on the literary and historical contexts of the book. For information on any passage of *Utopia*, Surtz's commentary is the first place to look. J. H. Lupton's 1895 edition of *Utopia* (Oxford) reprints the earliest English translation of the book, by Ralph Robinson (1551), together with the Latin text and a full and interesting commentary. Another massive commentary is found in the Latin-French edition by André Prévost (Paris, 1978).

Utopia participates in a sort of dialogue with earlier (and later) works of political thought. The Greek and Roman works in this dialogue, as well as the other classical works to which More alludes, are found in most libraries in the bilingual editions of the Loeb Classical Library. These are the editions quoted in the notes to this volume, except in the case of Aristotle's *Politics*, where we quote from the masterful edition by Ernest Barker (Oxford, 1948), and Plato's *Republic* and *Laws*, where we cite the engaging and handy Penguin translations: *The Republic*, trans. H. D. P. Lee, 2nd edn (1974); *The Laws*, trans. Trevor J. Saunders (1970). Passages in the works of More's fellow humanist Erasmus often provide the best gloss on passages of *Utopia*. Most of the major works are now available in the *Collected Works of Erasmus*, issuing from the University of Toronto Press (1974–). For *The Praise of Folly*, though, the translation by Hoyt Hopewell Hudson (Princeton, 1941) is handier and more attractive, and so we quote from it.

For the context of *Utopia* in Renaissance political thought, see Quentin Skinner, *The Foundations of Modern Political Thought*, 2 vols. (Cambridge, 1978). The history of utopian literature is massively treated by Frank E. and Fritzie P. Manuel, *Utopian Thought in the Western World* (Cambridge, Mass., 1979). On the history of More's time, see C. S. L. Davies, *Peace, Print and Protestantism 1450–1558*, The Paladin History of England (Frogmore, St Albans, Herts, 1977), or G. R. Elton, *Reform and Reformation: England, 1509–1558*, The New History of England, II (London and Cambridge, Mass., 1977); and, on the social problems addressed in *Utopia*, Joyce Youings, *Sixteenth-Century England*, The Pelican Social History of Britain (Harmondsworth, Middlesex, 1984).

The most influential books on *Utopia* are Hexter's brilliant little *More's 'Utopia': The Biography of an Idea* (1952; rpt with an epilogue,

New York, 1965), and two 1957 books by Surtz: *The Praise of Pleasure: Philosophy, Education, and Communism in More's Utopia* (Cambridge, Mass.) and *The Praise of Wisdom: A Commentary on the Religious and Moral Problems and Backgrounds of St Thomas More's 'Utopia'* (Chicago). Both contain a wealth of illuminating contextual information – much of which is, however (like much of the substance of Hexter's book), incorporated into the Yale *Utopia* (see above). Robert P. Adams, *The Better Part of Valor: More, Erasmus, Colet, and Vives, on Humanism, War, and Peace, 1496–1535* (Seattle, 1962), links *Utopia* to Erasmian pacifism. George M. Logan, *The Meaning of More's 'Utopia'* (Princeton, 1983), is primarily concerned with the relation between *Utopia* and classical and Renaissance political philosophy. This is also the focus of Quentin Skinner, 'Sir Thomas More's *Utopia* and the language of Renaissance humanism', in *The Languages of Political Theory in Early-Modern Europe*, ed. Anthony Pagden (Cambridge, 1987), pp. 123–57. Elizabeth McCutcheon shows how much More's book yields to close stylistic analysis: see *My Dear Peter: The 'Ars Poetica' and Hermeneutics for More's 'Utopia'* (Angers, 1983). She is particularly acute on More's use of the paradoxical tradition of *serio ludere*. *Essential Articles for the Study of Thomas More*, ed. R. S. Sylvester and G. P. Marc'hadour (Hamden, Conn., 1977), reprints a number of the best articles on *Utopia* and other works by More, and on facets of More's biography. The quarterly *Moreana* publishes articles on More, reviews scholarship on him, and reports the many and varied activities of the global circle of More scholars and admirers.

CONCERNING THE BEST
STATE OF A COMMONWEALTH
AND THE NEW ISLAND
OF UTOPIA

A Truly Golden Handbook,
No Less Beneficial than Entertaining,
by the Most Distinguished and Eloquent Author
THOMAS MORE
Citizen and Sheriff of the Famous City
of London

THOMAS MORE TO PETER GILES,
GREETINGS[1]

My dear Peter Giles, I am almost ashamed to be sending you after nearly a year this little book about the Utopian commonwealth which I'm sure you expected in less than six weeks.[2] For, as you were well aware, I faced no problem in finding my materials, and had no reason to ponder the arrangement of them.[3] All I had to do was repeat what you and I together heard Raphael[4] describe. By the same token, there was no occasion for me to labour over the style, since what he said, being extempore and informal, couldn't be couched in fancy terms.[5] And besides, as you know, he's a man better versed in Greek than in Latin;[6] so that my language would be nearer the truth, the closer it approached to his casual simplicity. Truth in fact is the only quality at which I should have aimed, or did aim, in writing this book.

I confess, friend Peter, that having all these materials ready to hand made my own contribution so slight that there was hardly anything at all for me to do. Thinking through this topic from the beginning and disposing it in proper order might have demanded a lot of time and work even if a man were not deficient in talent and learning. And then if the matter had to be set forth with eloquence,

---

[1] In the first edition of *Utopia*, this letter was called the 'preface' of the work; this is also its running title in the 1518 editions. On Giles (*c.* 1486–1533), see p. 9 and, on his role in the genesis of *Utopia*, Introduction, p. xvi.

[2] On the chronology, see Introduction, pp. xvi–xvii.

[3] Finding materials, disposing them in the proper order and couching them in the appropriate style are the three steps of literary composition (*inventio, dispositio, elocutio*), as that subject is treated in the classical textbooks of rhetoric and their medieval and Renaissance successors.

[4] I.e., Raphael Hythloday. His given name links him with the archangel Raphael, traditionally a guide and healer. (On his surname, see p. 5n.)

[5] Rhetorical theory identified three levels of style: the grand, the middle, and the plain. This sentence hints that *Utopia* is written in the plain style – according to theory, the appropriate one for philosophical dialogue.

[6] Knowledge of Greek was still uncommon among humanists in the early sixteenth century, and thus carried a good deal of status in their circles. Greek studies had been More's own preoccupation as a scholar in the decade leading up to *Utopia*.

3

not just factually, there's no way I could have done that, however hard I worked, for however long a time. But now when I was relieved of all these problems, over which I could have sweated forever, there was nothing for me to do but simply write down what I had heard. Well, little as it was, that task was rendered almost impossible by my many other obligations. Most of my day is given to the law – pleading some cases, hearing others, compromising others, and deciding still others. I have to visit this man because of his official position and that man because of his lawsuit; and so almost the whole day is devoted to other people's business and what's left over to my own; and then for myself – that is, my studies – there's nothing left.

For when I get home, I have to talk with my wife, chatter with my children, and consult with the servants. All these matters I consider part of my business, since they have to be done unless a man wants to be a stranger in his own house. Besides, everyone is bound to bear himself as agreeably as he can towards those whom nature or chance or his own choice has made the companions of his life. But of course he mustn't spoil them with his familiarity, or by overindulgence turn the servants into his masters. And so, amid these concerns, the day, the month and the year slip away.

What time do I find to write, then? Especially since I still have taken no account of sleeping or even of eating, to which many people devote as much time as to sleep itself, which devours almost half of our lives. My own time is only what I steal from sleeping and eating.[7] It isn't very much, but it's something, and so I've finally been able to finish our *Utopia*, even though belatedly, and I'm sending it to you now. I hope, my dear Peter, that you'll read it over and let me know if you find anything that I've overlooked. Though I'm not really afraid of having forgotten anything important – I wish my judgement and learning were up to my memory, which isn't too bad – still, I don't feel so sure of it that I would swear I've missed nothing.

For my servant John Clement[8] has raised a great doubt in my

---

[7] More's sixteenth-century biographer Thomas Stapleton says that he slept four or five hours a night, rising at 2 am. See *The Life and Illustrious Martyrdom of Sir Thomas More*, trans. Philip E. Hallett, ed. E. E. Reynolds (London, 1966), p. 28. Claiming that a book was composed in odd hours or inopportune circumstances was conventional, but in More's case there is no reason to doubt that the convention corresponded to fact.

[8] John Clement (d. 1572) was one of the first students of St Paul's School, the humanist grammar school founded by John Colet about 1509. By 1514 he had entered More's household as servant and pupil; in later life he became a respected physician.

mind. As you know, he was there with us, for I always want him to be present at conversations where there's profit to be gained. (And one of these days I expect we'll get a fine crop of learning from this young sprout, who's already made excellent progress in Greek as well as Latin.) Anyhow, as I recall matters, Hythloday[9] said the bridge over the Anyder at Amaurot was five hundred paces long; but my John says that is two hundred paces too much – that in fact the river is barely three hundred paces wide there. So I beg you, consult your memory. If your recollection agrees with his, I'll yield to the two of you, and confess myself mistaken. But if you don't recall the point, I'll follow my own memory and keep my present figure. For, as I've taken particular pains to avoid untruths in the book, so, if anything is in doubt, I'd rather make an honest mistake than say what I don't believe. In short, I'd rather be truthful than correct.

Note the theological distinction between a deliberate lie and an untruth[10]

But the whole matter can easily be cleared up if you'll ask Raphael about it – either directly, if he's still in your neighbourhood, or else by letter. And I'm afraid you must do this anyway, because of another problem that has cropped up – whether through my fault, or yours, or Raphael's, I'm not sure. For it didn't occur to us to ask, nor to him to say, in what area of the New World Utopia is to be found. I wouldn't have missed hearing about this for a sizeable sum of money, for I'm quite ashamed not to know even the name of the ocean where this island lies about which I've written so much. Besides, there are various people here, and one in particular, a devout man and a professor of theology, who very much wants to go to Utopia.[11] His motive is not by any means idle curiosity, but rather a desire to foster and further the growth of our religion, which has made such a happy start there. To this end, he has decided to arrange to be sent there by the Pope, and even to be named Bishop to the Utopians. He feels no particular scruples about intriguing for

---

[9] From Greek *hythlos* ('idle talk', 'nonsense') plus *daios* ('knowing', 'cunning') or *daiein* ('to distribute'): hence 'expert in nonsense' or 'nonsense peddler'. Similarly, 'Anyder' and 'Amaurot' are from *anydros*, 'waterless', and *amauroton*, 'made dark or dim'.

[10] This 'theological distinction' is found not in the theological literature but in a late classical work well known to humanists, Aulus Gellius' *Attic Nights* (XI.xi). The marginal glosses are apparently by Giles, though Erasmus may also have had a hand in them (see p. 125 and note).

[11] A note in a 1624 edition of *Utopia* identifies this learned divine as Rowland Phillips, Warden of Merton College, Oxford. But there is nothing to support the identification, and the passage may simply be one of the book's jokes at the expense of theologians.

Office-seeking in a good cause this post, for he considers it a holy project, arising not from motives of glory or gain, but simply from religious zeal.

Therefore I beg you, my dear Peter, to get in touch with Hythloday – in person if you can, or by letters if he's gone – and make sure that my work contains nothing false and omits nothing true. It would probably be just as well to show him the book itself. If I've made a mistake, there's nobody better qualified to correct me; but even he cannot do it, unless he reads over my book. Besides, you will be able to discover in this way whether he's pleased or annoyed that I have written the book. If he has decided to write out his own story for himself, he may be displeased with me; and I should be sorry, too, if in publicising Utopia I had robbed him and his story of the flower of novelty.

The fretful judgements of men But to tell the truth, I'm still of two minds as to whether I should publish the book or not. For men's tastes are so various, the tempers of some are so severe, their minds so ungrateful, their judgements so foolish, that there seems no point in publishing a book, even if it's intended for their advantage, that they will receive only with contempt and ingratitude. Better simply to follow one's own natural inclinations, lead a merry, peaceful life, and ignore the vexing problems of publication. Most men know nothing of learning; many despise it. The clod rejects as too difficult whatever isn't cloddish. The pedant dismisses as mere trifling anything that isn't stuffed with obsolete words. Some readers approve only of ancient authors; most men like their own writing best of all. Here's a man so solemn *Men who can't stand satire, he calls insipid* he won't allow a shadow of levity, and there's one so insipid of taste that he can't endure the salt of a little wit. Some dullards dread satire as a man bitten by a hydrophobic dog dreads water; some are so changeable that they like one thing when they're seated and another when they're standing.[12]

Those people lounge around the taverns, and as they swill their ale pass judgement on the intelligence of writers. With complete assurance they condemn every author by his writings, just as they think best, plucking each one, as it were, by the beard. But they *A saying* themselves remain safe – out of range, so to speak. No use trying to

---

[12] The last phrase echoes the *Invective against Cicero* (IV.7) attributed to the first-century BC Roman historian Sallust; the paragraph as a whole resembles Erasmus' complaints, in his letter to Maarten van Dorp, about ill-natured readers of *The Praise of Folly* (*CWE*, III, 129).

lay hold of them; they're shaved so close, there's not so much as the hair of an honest man to catch them by.

Finally, some men are so ungrateful that even though they're delighted with a work, they don't like the author any better because of it. They are no different from rude, ungrateful guests who, after *A neat comparison* they have stuffed themselves with a splendid dinner, go off, carrying their full bellies homeward without a word of thanks to the host who invited them. A fine task, providing at your own expense a banquet for men of such finicky palates and such various tastes, who will reward you with thanks of that sort.

At any rate, my dear Peter, will you take up with Hythloday the matter I spoke of? After I've heard from him, I'll look over the whole question again. But since I've already taken the pains to write up the subject, it's too late to be wise. In the matter of publication, I hope we can have Hythloday's approval; after that, I'll follow the advice of my friends – and especially yours. Farewell, my dear Peter Giles; my regards to your excellent wife. Love me as you have always done; I remain more fond of you than ever.

THE BEST STATE OF A COMMONWEALTH,
A DISCOURSE BY THE EXTRAORDINARY
RAPHAEL HYTHLODAY, AS RECORDED BY
THE NOTED THOMAS MORE,
CITIZEN AND SHERIFF[1]
OF THE FAMOUS
CITY OF BRITAIN, LONDON
BOOK I

The most invincible King of England, Henry the Eighth of that name, a prince adorned with the royal virtues beyond any other,[2] had recently some differences of no slight import with Charles, the most serene Prince of Castile,[3] and sent me into Flanders as his spokesman to discuss and settle them. I was companion and associ-

Cuthbert Tunstall ate to that incomparable man Cuthbert Tunstall, whom the king has recently created Master of the Rolls, to everyone's great satisfaction.[4] I will say nothing in praise of this man, not because I fear the judgement of a friend might be questioned, but because his integrity and learning are greater than I can describe and too well known everywhere to need my commendation – unless I would, according

Adage to the proverb, 'show the sun with a lantern'.

Those appointed by the prince to deal with us, all excellent men,

---

[1] More had been Undersheriff of London since 1510. His principal duty was to act as a judge in the Sheriff's Court (a city court that heard a wide variety of cases).

[2] When he succeeded to the throne in 1509 at the age of seventeen, Henry appeared to be something very close to the humanist ideal of a cultivated, just and peace-loving monarch, and More had enthusiastically heralded his accession in several Latin poems (*CW*, III, Part 2, 101–17). By 1516, however, this view had been considerably undermined, especially by the king's fondness for martial (not yet marital) adventure.

[3] The disputes between the two nations were commercial ones, especially over tariffs. Charles was grandson of the Emperor Maximilian I and Duke of Burgundy after his father's death in 1506. He became, nominally though not formally, Prince of Castile after the death of Ferdinand II (23 January 1516), and Holy Roman Emperor in 1519.

[4] A royal commission of 7 May 1515 appointed five commissioners, including More, with Tunstall as their chief. Tunstall (1474–1559) was created Master of the Rolls (principal clerk of the Chancery Court) and Vice-Chancellor of the realm on 12 May 1516.

8

met us at Bruges by pre-arrangement. Their head man and leader was the Mayor of Bruges, a most distinguished person. But their main speaker and guiding spirit was Georges de Themsecke, the Provost of Cassel, a man eloquent by nature as well as by training, very learned in the law, and most skilful in diplomatic affairs through his ability and long practice. After we had met several times, certain points remained on which we could not come to agreement; so they adjourned the meeting[5] and went to Brussels for some days to consult their prince in person.

Meanwhile, since my business required it, I went to Antwerp. Of those who visited me while I was there, Peter Giles was more wel- *Peter Giles* come to me than any of the others. He was a native of Antwerp, a man of high reputation, already appointed to a good position and worthy of the very best: I hardly know a young man of more learning or better character. Apart from being cultured, virtuous and courteous to all, with his intimates he is so open, trustworthy, loyal and affectionate that it would be hard to find another friend like him anywhere. No man is more modest or more frank; none better combines simplicity with wisdom. His conversation is so pleasant, and so witty without malice, that the ardent desire I felt to see my native country, my wife and my children (from whom I had been separated more than four months) was much eased by his agreeable company and pleasant talk.

One day after I had heard Mass at Nôtre Dame, the most beautiful and most popular church in Antwerp, I was about to return to my quarters when I happened to see him talking with a stranger, a man of quite advanced years. The stranger had a sunburned face, a long beard and a cloak hanging loosely from his shoulders; from his face and dress, I took him to be a ship's captain. When Peter saw me, he approached and greeted me. As I was about to return his greeting, he drew me aside and, indicating the stranger, said, 'Do you see that man? I was just on the point of bringing him to you.'

'He would have been very welcome on your behalf,' I answered.

'And on his own too, if you knew him,' said Peter, 'for there is no man alive today can tell you so much about strange peoples and unexplored lands; and I know that you're always greedy for such information.'

[5] On or before 21 July 1515. See Introduction, p. xvi.

'In that case,' said I, 'my guess wasn't a bad one, for at first glance I supposed he was a skipper.'

'Then you're off the mark,' he replied, 'for his sailing has not been like that of Palinurus, but more that of Ulysses, or rather of Plato.[6] This man, who is named Raphael – his family name is Hythloday – knows a good deal of Latin and is particularly learned in Greek. He studied Greek more than Latin because his main interest is philosophy, and in that field he found that the Romans have left us nothing very valuable except certain works of Seneca and Cicero.[7] Being eager to see the world, he bestowed on his brothers the patrimony to which he was entitled at home (for he is Portuguese by birth),[8] and took service with Amerigo Vespucci. He accompanied Vespucci on the last three of his four voyages, accounts of which are now common reading everywhere;[9] but on the last voyage, he did not return home with the commander. After much persuasion and expostulation he got Amerigo's permission to be one of the twenty-four men who were left in a garrison at the farthest point of the last voyage. Being marooned in this way was altogether agreeable to him, as he was more eager to pursue his travels than afraid of death. He would often say, "The man who has no

Aphorism grave is covered by the sky", and "The road to heaven is equally short from all places."[10] Yet this frame of mind would have cost him dear, if God had not been gracious to him. After Vespucci's

[6] Palinurus was Aeneas' pilot: he dozed at the helm and fell overboard (*Aeneid* v.833–61, vi.337–83). Ulysses' reputation as a man who saw many cities and knew men's minds is based on the first few lines of the *Odyssey*. According to the Life of Plato by Diogenes Laertius (fl. third century AD), Plato travelled widely in the Mediterranean world (*Lives of Eminent Philosophers* iii.6,18–19).

[7] This opinion is echoed in More's 1518 Letter to Oxford (*Selected Letters*, p. 100). Seneca was a Stoic; and though Cicero styled himself an adherent of the sceptical philosophy associated with the later phase of the Platonic Academy, his sympathies in ethical and political theory lay mainly with the Stoics, whose views he often rehearsed at length. Hythloday's own views are permeated by Stoic ideas.

[8] Hythloday's nationality links him with several of the great explorers of the period, who were either Portuguese or sponsored by the King of Portugal.

[9] Two Latin accounts of the voyages of the Florentine explorer Amerigo Vespucci (1451–1512), who sailed for the King of Portugal, were published about 1504: *New World* and *The Four Voyages of Amerigo Vespucci. Utopia* exhibits parallels with both. *Four Voyages* tells that Vespucci left twenty-four men at the farthest point of his fourth voyage (in Martin Walseemüller, *Cosmographiae Introductio* (Ann Arbor, Mich., 1966), pp. 149–50).

[10] The first of these sayings is quoted from the epic poem by Seneca's nephew Lucan, *Pharsalia* (vii.819); the second is adapted from Cicero (*Tusculan Disputations* i.xliii.104).

departure he travelled through many countries with five companions from the garrison. At last, by strange good fortune, he got via Ceylon to Calicut,[11] where by good luck he found some Portuguese ships; and so, beyond anyone's expectation, he returned to his own country.'

When Peter had told me this, I thanked him for his kindness in introducing me to a man whose conversation he hoped I would enjoy, and then I turned towards Raphael. After greeting one another and exchanging the usual civilities of strangers upon their first meeting, we all went to my house. There in the garden we sat down on a bench covered with grassy turf to talk together.

He told us that after Vespucci sailed away, he and his companions who had stayed behind in the garrison often met with the people of the countryside, and by ingratiating speeches gradually won their friendship. Before long they came to dwell with them safely and even affectionately. The prince also gave them his favour (I have forgotten his name and that of his country), furnishing Raphael and his five companions not only with ample provisions, but with means for travelling – rafts when they went by water, wagons when they went by land. In addition, he sent with them a most trusty guide who was to introduce and recommend them to such other princes as they wanted to visit. After many days' journey, he said, they came to towns and cities, and to commonwealths that were both populous and not badly governed.

To be sure, under the equator and as far on both sides of the line as the sun moves, there lie vast empty deserts, scorched with the perpetual heat. The whole region is desolate and squalid, grim and uncultivated, inhabited by wild beasts, serpents and men no less wild and dangerous than the beasts themselves. But as they went on, conditions gradually grew milder. The heat was less fierce, the earth greener, the creatures less savage. At last they reached people, cities and towns which not only traded among themselves and with their neighbours, but even carried on commerce by sea and land with remote countries. After that, he said, they were able to visit different lands in every direction, for he and his companions were welcome as passengers aboard any ship about to make a journey.

The first vessels they saw were flat-bottomed, he said, with sails

---

[11] Calicut is a seaport on the west coast of India.

made of papyrus-reeds and wicker, occasionally of leather. Farther on they found ships with pointed keels and canvas sails, in every respect like our own. The seamen were skilled in managing wind and water; but they were most grateful to him, Raphael said, for showing them the use of the compass, of which they had been ignorant. For that reason they had formerly sailed with great timidity, and only in summer. Now they have such trust in the compass that they no longer fear winter at all, and tend to be rash rather than cautious. There is some danger that through their imprudence this discovery, which they thought would be so advantageous to them, may become the cause of much mischief.

It would take too long to repeat all that Raphael told us he had observed in various places, nor would it altogether serve our present purpose. Perhaps on another occasion we shall tell more about the things that are most profitable, especially the wise and sensible institutions that he observed among the civilised nations. We asked him many eager questions about such things, and he answered us willingly enough. We made no inquiries, however, about monsters, which are the routine of travellers' tales. Scyllas, ravenous Celaenos, man-eating Lestrygonians[12] and that sort of monstrosity you can hardly avoid, but to find governments wisely established and sensibly ruled is not so easy. While he told us of many ill-considered usages in these new-found nations, he also described quite a few other customs from which our own cities, nations, races and kingdoms might take lessons in order to correct their errors. These I shall discuss in another place, as I said. Now I intend to relate only what he told us about the manners and institutions of the Utopians,[13] first explaining the occasion that led him to speak of that commonwealth. Raphael had been discoursing very thoughtfully on the many errors and also the wiser institutions found both in that

---

[12] Scylla, a six-headed sea monster, appears in both the *Odyssey* (XII.73–100, 234–59) and the *Aeneid* (III.420–32). Celaeno, one of the Harpies (birds with women's faces), appears in the *Aeneid* (III.209–58). The Lestrygonians were gigantic cannibals in the *Odyssey* (X.76–132).

[13] At this point the dialogue suddenly goes off on a different tack. The account of Utopia is postponed; and the ensuing conversation includes, among other things, precisely those matters that More has just said he won't relate: Hythloday's descriptions of the practices of other new-found nations. As J. H. Hexter argues (*More's 'Utopia': The Biography of an Idea*, pp. 18–21; *CW*, IV, xviii–xx), it was almost certainly here that More opened a seam in the first version of *Utopia* to insert the additions that constitute the remainder of Book I. See Introduction, pp. xvi–xvii.

hemisphere and in this (as many of both sorts in one place as in the other), speaking as shrewdly about the manners and governments of each place he had briefly visited as if he had lived there all his life. Peter was amazed.

'My dear Raphael,' he said, 'I'm surprised that you don't enter some king's service; for I don't know of a single prince who wouldn't be glad to have you. Your learning and your knowledge of various countries and men would entertain him while your advice and supply of examples would be helpful at the counsel board. Thus you might advance your own interest agreeably and be of great use at the same time to all your relatives and friends.'

'About my relatives and friends,' he replied, 'I'm not much concerned, because I consider I've already done my duty by them. While still young and healthy, I distributed among my relatives and friends the possessions that most men do not part with till they're old and sick (and then only reluctantly, when they can no longer keep them). I think they should be content with this gift of mine, and not expect, far less insist, that for their sake I should enslave myself to any king whatever.'

'Well said,' Peter replied; 'but I do not mean that you should be in servitude to any king, only in his service.'

'The difference is only a matter of one syllable,' Raphael replied.

'All right,' said Peter, 'but whatever you call it, I do not see any other way in which you can be so useful to your friends or to the general public, in addition to making yourself happier.'

'Happier indeed!' exclaimed Raphael. 'Would a way of life so absolutely repellent to my spirit make my life happier? As it is now, I live as I please,[14] and I fancy very few courtiers, however splendid, can say that. As a matter of fact, there are so many men soliciting favours from the great that it will be no great loss if they have to do without me and a couple of others like me.'

Then I said, 'It is clear, my dear Raphael, that you seek neither wealth nor power, and indeed I prize and revere a man of your disposition no less than I do the greatest persons in the world. Yet I think if you would devote your time and energy to public affairs, you would be doing something worthy of a generous and truly philo-

---

[14] Hythloday paraphrases Cicero's definition of liberty, which occurs in a context similar to the present one (*On Moral Obligation* I.xx.69–70).

sophical nature, even if you did not much like it. You could best perform such a service by joining the council of some great prince,
whom you would incite to just and noble actions. I'm sure you would
do this if you held such an office, and your influence would be felt,
because a people's welfare or misery flows in a stream from their
prince as from a never-failing spring. Your learning is so full, even
if it weren't combined with experience, and your experience is so
great, even apart from your learning, that you would be an extraordinary counsellor to any king in the world.'

'You are twice mistaken, my dear More,' he replied, 'first in me
and then in the situation itself. I don't have the capacity you ascribe
to me, and if I had it in the highest degree, the public would not be
any better off if I bartered my peace of mind for some ruler's convenience. In the first place, most princes apply themselves to the arts of
war, in which I have neither interest nor ability, instead of to the
good arts of peace. They are generally more set on acquiring new
kingdoms by hook or crook than on governing well those they
already have. Moreover, the counsellors of kings are so wise already
that they don't need advice from anyone else – or at least they have
that opinion of themselves. At the same time they endorse and flatter
the most absurd statements of the prince's special favourites,
through whose influence they hope to stand well with the prince. It's
only natural, of course, that each man should think his own
opinions best: the old crow loves his fledgling and the ape his cub.

'Now in a court composed of people who envy everyone else and
admire only themselves, if a man should suggest something he had
read of in other ages or seen in practice elsewhere, the other counsellors would think their reputation for wisdom was endangered,
and henceforth they would look like simpletons, unless they could
find fault with his proposal. If all else failed, they would take refuge
in some remark like this: "The way we're doing it is the way we've
always done it, this custom was good enough for our fathers, and I
only hope we're as wise as they were." And with this deep thought
they would take their seats, as though they had said the last word on
the subject – implying, forsooth, that it would be a very dangerous
matter if a man were found to be wiser on any point than his forefathers were. As a matter of fact, we quietly neglect the best examples
they have left us; but if something better is proposed, we seize the
excuse of reverence for times past and cling to it desperately. Such

proud, obstinate, ridiculous judgements I have encountered many times, and once even in England.'

'What!' I asked, 'Were you ever in England?'

'Yes,' he answered, 'I spent several months there. It was not long after the revolt of the Cornishmen against the King had been put down with great slaughter of the poor folk involved.[15] During my stay I was deeply beholden to the reverend prelate John Cardinal Morton, Archbishop of Canterbury and also at that time Lord Chancellor of England.[16] He was a man, my dear Peter (for More knows about him and can tell what I'm going to say), as much respected for his wisdom and virtue as for his authority. He was of medium height, not bent over despite his age; his looks inspired respect, not fear. In conversation, he was not forbidding, though serious and grave. When petitioners came to him on business, he liked to test their spirit and presence of mind by speaking to them sharply, though not rudely. He liked to uncover these qualities, which were those of his own nature, as long as they were not carried to the point of effrontery; and he thought such men were best qualified to carry on business. His speech was polished and pointed, his knowledge of the law was great, he had a vast understanding and a prodigious memory, for he had improved excellent natural abilities by constant study and practice. At the time when I was in England, the King depended greatly on his advice, and he seemed the mainspring of all public affairs. He had left school for the court when scarcely more than a boy, had devoted all his life to important business, and had acquired from many changes of fortune and at great cost a supply of wisdom, which is not soon lost when so purchased.

'It happened one day when I was dining with him there was present a layman, learned in the laws of your country, who for some reason took occasion to praise the rigid execution of justice then *Of unjust laws* being practised on thieves. They were being executed everywhere, he said, with as many as twenty at a time being hanged on a single gallows.[17] And then he declared he could not understand how so

---

[15] Angered by Henry VII's rapacious taxation, an army of Cornishmen marched on London in 1497. They were defeated at the Battle of Blackheath and savagely slaughtered.

[16] More had deeply admired Morton (1420–1500) since serving as a page in his household. There is a similar portrait of him in *The History of King Richard III* (*CW*, II, 90–1).

[17] Holinshed the chronicler reports that, in the reign of Henry VIII alone, 72,000 thieves were hanged (*Holinshed's Chronicles [of] England, Scotland, and Ireland*, 6 vols. (London, 1807; rpt, New York, 1965), I, 314).

many thieves sprang up everywhere when so few of them escaped hanging. I ventured to speak freely before the Cardinal, and said, "There is no need to wonder: this way of punishing thieves goes beyond the call of justice, and is not in any case for the public good. The penalty is too harsh in itself, yet it isn't an effective deterrent. Simple theft is not so great a crime that it ought to cost a man his head, yet no punishment however severe can restrain men from robbery when they have no other way to eat. In this matter not only you in England but a good part of the world seem to imitate bad schoolmasters, who would rather whip their pupils than teach them.

How to reduce the number of thieves Severe and terrible punishments are enacted for theft, when it would be much better to enable every man to earn his own living, instead of being driven to the awful necessity of stealing and then dying for it."

'"Oh, we've taken care of all that", said the fellow. "There are the trades and there is farming by which men may make a living, unless they choose deliberately to do evil."

'"Oh no, you don't," I said, "you won't get out of it that way. We may overlook the cripples who come home from foreign and civil wars, as lately from the Cornish battle and before that from your wars with France.[18] These men, who have lost limbs in the service of king and country, are too shattered to follow their old trades and too old to learn new ones. But since wars occur only from time to time, let us, I say, overlook these men and see what happens every day. There are a great many noblemen who live idly like drones off the labour of others,[19] their tenants whom they bleed white by constantly raising their rents. (This is the only instance of their tightfistedness, because they are prodigal in everything else, ready to

[18] Since the dramatic date of the conversation is 1497 or shortly thereafter, Hythloday may refer to the relatively small number of casualties suffered by the English during the sporadic hostilities in France in 1489–92. But More is probably thinking of the heavier casualties of Henry VIII's French excursions of 1512–13.

[19] In the *Republic*, Socrates uses the same metaphor to describe the kind of monied individual who contributes nothing to society: 'Though he may have appeared to belong to the ruling class, surely in fact he was neither ruling, nor serving society in any other way; he was merely a consumer of goods ... Don't you think we can fairly call him a drone?' (VIII.552B–C). In general, Plato's characterisation of oligarchy seems to have provided More with a framework for organising his observations on the condition of England. An oligarchy is 'a society where it is wealth that counts, ... and in which political power is in the hands of the rich and the poor have no share of it' (VIII.550C). The 'worst defect' of such a society is that it generates functionless people (552A).

spend their way to the poorhouse.) What's more, these gentry drag around with them a great train of idle servants, who have never learned any trade by which they could make a living.[20] As soon as their master dies, or they themselves fall ill, they are promptly turned out of doors, for lords would rather support idlers than invalids, and the son is often unable to maintain as big a household as his father had, at least at first. Those who are turned out soon set about starving, unless they set about stealing. What else can they do? Then when a wandering life has taken the edge off their health and the gloss off their clothes, when their faces look pinched and their garments tattered, men of rank will not want to engage them. And country folk dare not do so, for they don't have to be told that one who has been raised softly to idle pleasures, who has been used to swaggering about like a bully with sword and buckler, is likely to look down on the whole neighbourhood and despise everybody else as beneath him. Such a man can't be put to work with spade and mattock; he will not serve a poor man laboriously for scant wages and sparse diet."

'"We ought to encourage these men in particular", said the lawyer. "In case of war the strength of our army depends on them because they have a bolder and nobler spirit than workmen and farmers have."

'"You may as well say that thieves should be encouraged for the sake of wars," I answered, "since you will never lack for thieves as long as you have men like these. Just as some thieves are not bad soldiers, some soldiers turn out to be pretty good robbers, so nearly are these two ways of life related.[21] But the custom of keeping too many retainers, though frequent here, is not yours alone, it is common to almost all nations. France suffers from an even more grievous plague. Even in peacetime, if you can call it peace, the whole country is crowded with foreign mercenaries, imported on the same principle that you've given for your noblemen keeping idle servants.[22]

---

[20] Some of these retainers were household servants; others constituted the remnants of the private armies which, in a feudal society, followed every lord. In the reign of Henry VII the latter kind of retaining was sharply curtailed.

[21] The close kinship between the professions of soldier and robber is a frequent theme of Erasmus and other humanists. See, for example, Erasmus' *Complaint of Peace* (*CWE*, XXVII, 316–17).

[22] In the early sixteenth century, French infantry forces were mainly Swiss and German mercenaries.

Wise fools[23] have a saying that the public safety depends on having
ready a strong army, preferably of veteran soldiers. They think
The mischief of inexperienced men are not reliable, and they sometimes hunt out
standing armies pretexts for war, just so they may have trained soldiers; hence men's
throats are cut for no reason – lest, as Sallust neatly puts it, 'hand
and spirit grow dull through lack of practice'.[24] But France has
learned to her cost how pernicious it is to feed such beasts. The
examples of the Romans, the Carthaginians, the Syrians and many
other peoples show the same thing; for not only their governments
but their fields and even their cities were ruined more than once
by their own standing armies.[25] Besides, this preparedness is unnecessary: not even the French soldiers, practised in arms from
their cradles, can boast of having often got the best of your raw
recruits.[26] I shall say no more on this point, lest I seem to flatter
present company. At any rate, neither your town workmen nor your
rough farm labourers, as long as they're not weakened by some accident or cowed by extreme poverty, seem to be much afraid of those
idle retainers. So you need not fear that retainers, once strong and
vigorous (for that's the only sort the gentry deign to corrupt), but
now soft and flabby because of their idle, effeminate life, would be
weakened if they were taught practical crafts to earn their living and
trained to manly labour. Anyway, I cannot think it's in the public
interest to maintain for the emergency of war such a vast multitude
of people who trouble and disturb the peace: you never have war
unless you choose it, and peace is always more to be considered than
war. Yet this is not the only force driving men to thievery. There is
another that, as I see it, applies specially to you Englishmen."

'"What is that?" asked the Cardinal.

'"Your sheep," I replied, "that commonly are so meek and eat so
little; now, as I hear, they have become so greedy and fierce that they

---

[23] *Morosophi* (transliterated from Greek). The modern word 'sophomore' is the same
combination reversed.

[24] Paraphrased from *Catiline* XVI.3.

[25] The Romans fought full-scale wars against runaway gladiators, and the Carthaginians against mutinous mercenaries; the 'Syrians' are perhaps Turks and Egyptians
who enrolled captured Christians in their armies under the title of janizaries and
mamelukes.

[26] Past English victories over the French included Crécy (1346), Poitiers (1356) and
Henry V's triumph at Agincourt (1415).

devour men themselves.[27] They devastate and depopulate fields, houses and towns. For in whatever parts of the land sheep yield the finest and thus the most expensive wool, there the nobility and gentry, yes, and even some abbots though otherwise holy men, are not content with the old rents that the land yielded to their predecessors. Living in idleness and luxury without doing society any good no longer satisfies them; they have to do positive evil. For they leave no land free for the plough: they enclose every acre for pasture; they destroy houses and abolish towns, keeping only the churches – and those for sheep-barns. And as if enough of your land were not already wasted on forests and game-preserves, these worthy men turn all human habitations and cultivated fields back to wilderness. Thus one greedy, insatiable glutton, a frightful plague to his native country, may enclose many thousands of acres within a single hedge. The tenants are dismissed and compelled, by trickery or brute force or constant harassment, to sell their belongings. One way or another, these wretched people – men, women, husbands, wives, orphans, widows, parents with little children and entire families (poor but numerous, since farming requires many hands) – are forced to move out. They leave the only homes familiar to them, and can find no place to go. Since they must leave at once without waiting for a proper buyer, they sell for a pittance all their household goods, which would not bring much in any case. When that little money is gone (and it's soon spent in wandering from place to place), what remains for them but to steal, and so be hanged – justly, you'd say! – or to wander and beg? And yet if they go tramping, they are jailed as idle vagrants. They would be glad to work, but they can find no one who will hire them. There is no need for farm labour, in which they have been trained, when there is no land left to be ploughed. One herdsman or shepherd can look after a flock of beasts large enough to stock an area that would require many hands if it were to be ploughed and sowed.

‘"This enclosing has led to sharply rising food prices in many districts. Also, the price of raw wool has risen so much that poor

[27] This vivid image capsulises the social dislocation brought about by enclosure – the practice of private landlords in buying up and fencing in common lands which from time immemorial had been shared by everybody. Making more money out of wool was the landlords' major motive; a social consequence was the removal of peasants and yeomen from the land they had cultivated. They were pauperised or, drifting into the cities, proletarianised.

people who used to make cloth can no longer afford it, and so great numbers are forced from work to idleness. One reason is that after so much new pasture-land was enclosed, rot killed a great many of the sheep – as though God were punishing greed by sending on the beasts a murrain that rightly should have fallen on the owners! But even if the number of sheep should increase greatly, their price will not fall a penny, because the wool trade, though it can't be called a monopoly because it isn't in the hands of a single person, is concentrated in so few hands (an oligopoly, you might say), and these so rich, that the owners are never pressed to sell until they have a mind to, and that is only when they can get their price.

' "For the same reason other kinds of livestock are also priced exorbitantly, the more so because, with cottages being torn down and farming in decay, nobody is left to breed the cattle. These rich men will not breed calves as they do lambs, but buy them lean and cheap, fatten them in their pastures, and then sell them dear. I don't think the full impact of this bad system has yet been felt. We know these dealers hurt consumers where the fattened cattle are sold. But when, over a period of time, they keep buying beasts from other localities faster than they can be bred, a gradually diminishing supply where they are bought will inevitably lead to shortages. So your island, which seemed specially fortunate in this matter, will be ruined by the crass avarice of a few. For the high cost of living causes the rich man to dismiss as many retainers as he can from his household; and what, I ask, can these men do but rob or beg? And a man of courage is more likely to steal than to cringe.

' "To make this hideous poverty worse, it exists side by side with wanton luxury.[28] The servants of noblemen, tradespeople, even some farmers – people of every social rank – are given to ostentatious dress and gluttonous eating. Look at the cook-shops, the bawdy houses and those other places just as bad, the wine-bars and beer-halls. Look at all the crooked games of chance like dice, cards, backgammon, tennis, bowling and quoits, in which money slips away so fast. Don't all these pastimes lead their addicts straight to robbery?

---

[28] Extravagant display was not in fact characteristic of the reign of the parsimonious Henry VII (the period in which Hythloday is supposed to be addressing Cardinal Morton). More seems to be projecting on to the earlier period the taste for display associated with the reign of Henry VIII. Of course to an ascetic like More, all courts would appear overindulgent.

Banish these blights, make those who have ruined farmhouses and villages restore them or rent them to someone who will rebuild. Restrict the right of the rich to buy up anything and everything, and then to exercise a kind of monopoly.[29] Let fewer people be brought up in idleness. Let agriculture be restored, and the wool-manufacture revived, so there will be useful work for those now idle, whether those whom poverty has already made thieves or those who are only vagabonds and layabouts now, but are bound to become thieves in the future.

'"If you don't try to cure these evils, it is futile to boast of your severity in punishing theft. Your policy may look superficially like justice, but in reality it is neither just nor practical. If you allow young folk to be abominably brought up and their characters corrupted, little by little, from childhood; and if then you punish them as grownups for committing the crimes to which their training has inclined them, what else is this, I ask, but first making them thieves and then punishing them for it?"

'As I was speaking thus, the lawyer had prepared his answer, choosing the solemn style of disputants who are better at summing up than at replying, and who like to show off their memory. So he said to me, "You have talked very well for a stranger, but you have heard more than you've been able to understand correctly. I will make the matter clear to you in a few words. First, I will summarise what you said; then I will show how you have been misled by ignorance of our customs; finally, I will demolish all your arguments and dissolve them. And so to begin where I promised, on four points you seemed to me —"

'"Hold your tongue," said the Cardinal, "for you won't be finished in a few words if this is the way you start. We will spare you the trouble of answering now, and reserve the pleasure of your reply till our next meeting, which will be tomorrow if your affairs and Raphael's permit it. Meanwhile, my dear Raphael, I'd be glad to hear why you think theft should not be punished with death, or what other punishment you think would be more suitable. For I'm sure even you don't think it should go unpunished entirely. Even as it is, fear of death does not restrain the malefactors; once they were sure

Illustrates the Cardinal's way of interrupting a babbler

---

[29] A number of laws to control gambling and ale-houses, restrict monopolies and provide for the rebuilding of towns and the restoration of pastures to tillage were in fact passed, with small result, in the reigns of both Henry VII and Henry VIII.

of their lives, as you propose, what force or fear could withhold them? They would look on a lighter penalty as an invitation to commit more crimes, almost a reward."

"'It seems to me, most kind and reverend father," I said, "that it's altogether unjust that a man should lose his life for the loss of someone's money. Nothing in the world that fortune can bestow is equal in value to a man's life. If they say the thief suffers, not for the money, but for violation of justice and transgression of laws, then this extreme justice should properly be called extreme injury.[30] We *Manlian edicts* ought not to approve of these fierce Manlian edicts that invoke the *from Livy* sword for the smallest violations.[31] Nor should we accept the Stoic view that all crimes are equal,[32] as if there were no difference between killing a man and taking a coin from him. If equity means anything, there is no proportion or relation at all between these two crimes. God has said, 'Thou shalt not kill'; shall we kill so readily for the theft of a bit of small change? Perhaps it will be argued that God's law against killing does not apply where human laws allow it. But what then prevents men from making other laws in the same way, perhaps legalising rape, adultery and perjury? If mutual consent to human laws entitles men by special decree to exempt their agents from divine law and allows them to kill where he has given us no example, what is this but preferring the law of man to the law of God? The result will be that in every situation men will decide for themselves how far it suits them to observe the laws of God. The law of Moses is harsh and severe, as for an enslaved and stubborn people, but it punishes theft with a fine, not death.[33] Let us not think that in his new law of mercy, where he rules us as a father rules his children, God has given us greater license to be cruel to one another.

"'These are the reasons why I think it wrong to put thieves to death. But everybody knows how absurd and even dangerous it is to punish theft and murder alike. If he sees that theft carries the same

---

[30] The phrase echoes the adage *summum ius, summa iniuria* (quoted by Cicero, *On Moral Obligation* I.x.33), which has a long history in discussions of equity.

[31] According to Livy, the Roman general Manlius (fourth century BC) executed his own son for violating one of his ordinances (*From the Founding of the City* VIII.vii.1–22). 'Manlian edicts' was therefore proverbial for inexorable decrees.

[32] Cicero ridicules this Stoic paradox (*On the Supreme Good and Evil* IV.ix.21–3, xxvii.75–xxviii.77).

[33] The Mosaic law on theft is spelled out in the first verses of Exodus 22. It provides various penalties for theft, but nowhere death. This law is contrasted with the 'new law' of Christ, under which England is supposed to be operating.

penalty as murder, the thief will be encouraged to kill the victim whom otherwise he would only have robbed. When the punishment is the same, murder is safer, since one conceals both crimes by killing the witness. Thus while we try to terrify thieves with extreme cruelty, we really urge them to kill the innocent.

'"Now since you ask what more suitable punishment can be found, in my judgement it would be far easier to find a better one than a worse. Why should we question the value of the punishments long used by the ancient Romans, who were most expert in the arts of government? They condemned those convicted of heinous crimes to work in shackles for the rest of their lives in stone quarries and mines. But of all the alternatives, I prefer the method I observed in my Persian travels among the people commonly called the Poly- *The Polylerite* lerites.[34] They are a sizeable nation, not badly governed, free and *society near the Persians* subject only to their own laws, except that they pay annual tribute to the Persian Shah. Living far from the sea, they are nearly surrounded by mountains; and as they are content with the products of their own land (it is by no means unfruitful), they have little to do with other nations, and are not much visited. By ancient tradition, they make no effort to enlarge their boundaries, and easily protect themselves behind their mountains by paying tribute to their overlord. Thus they fight no wars, and live in a comfortable rather than a glorious manner, more contented than ambitious or famous. Indeed, I think they are hardly known by name to anyone but their next-door neighbours.

'"In their land, whoever is found guilty of theft must make resti- *To be noted by us,* tution to the owner, not (as elsewhere) to the prince;[35] they think the *who do otherwise* prince has no more right to the stolen goods than the thief. If the stolen property has disappeared, its value is estimated, and restoration is made from the thief's belongings. All the rest is handed over to his wife and children, while the thief himself is sentenced to hard labour.

'"Unless their crimes were compounded with atrocities, thieves are neither imprisoned nor shackled, but go freely and unguarded about their work on public projects. If they shirk and do their jobs

---

[34] More's coinage from *polus* ('much') plus *leros* ('nonsense'): 'the People of Much Nonsense'.

[35] Erasmus also condemns this common European practice, in *The Education of a Christian Prince (CWE, xxvii, 270)*.

slackly, they are not chained, but they are whipped. If they work hard, they undergo no humiliation, except that at night after roll call they are locked in their dormitories. Apart from constant labour, their life is not uncomfortable. As workers for the commonwealth, they are decently fed out of the public stores, though exact arrangements vary from place to place. In some districts they are supported by alms. Unreliable as this support may seem, the Polylerites are so charitable that no way is found more rewarding. In other places, public revenues are set aside for their support, or a special tax is levied; and sometimes they do not do public work, but anyone in need of workmen can go to the market and hire a convict by the day at a set rate, a little less than that for free men. If they are lazy, it is lawful to whip them. Thus the convicts are kept occupied, and each brings a little profit into the public treasury beyond the cost of his keep.

'"All of them, and only they, are dressed in clothes of the same distinctive colour. Their hair is not shaved off, but trimmed close about the ears, and the tip of one ear is cut off. Their friends are allowed to give them food, drink, or clothing, as long as it is of the proper colour; but to give them money is death, to both the giver and the taker. It is just as serious a crime for any free man to take money from them, for whatever reason; and it is also a capital crime for any of these slaves (as the condemned are called) to touch weapons. In each district of the country they are required to wear a special badge. It is a capital crime to discard the badge, to go beyond one's own district, or to talk with a slave of another district. Plotting escape is no more secure than escape itself: for any slave to know of an escape-plot is death, and for a free man, slavery. On the other hand, there are rewards for informers – money for a free man, freedom for a slave, and for both of them pardon and amnesty. Thus it can never be safer to persist in an illicit scheme than to repent of it.

'"These then are their policies in this matter. It is clear how mild and practical they are, for the aim of the punishment is to destroy vices and save men. The criminals are treated so that they necessarily become good, and they have the rest of their lives to atone for the wrong they have done. There is so little danger of recidivism that travellers going from one part of the country to another think slaves the most reliable guides, changing them at the boundary of each district. The slaves have no means of committing robbery, since they are unarmed, and any money in their possession is evidence of a

Yet modern servants exult in livery of the same sort

crime. If caught, they would be instantly punished, and there is no hope of escape anywhere. Since every bit of a slave's clothing is unlike the usual clothing of the country, how could one escape, unless he fled naked? And even then his cropped ear would give him away. Might not the slaves form a conspiracy against the government? Perhaps. But slaves of a single district could hardly expect to succeed unless they involved in their plot slave-gangs from many other districts. And that is impossible, since they are not allowed to meet or talk together, or even to greet one another. No one would risk a plot when they know joining is so dangerous to the participant and betrayal so profitable to the informer. Besides, no one is quite without hope of gaining his freedom eventually if he accepts his punishment in a spirit of patient obedience, and gives promise of future good conduct. Indeed, every year some are pardoned as a reward for submissive behaviour."

'When I had finished this account, I added that I saw no reason why this policy could not be adopted even in England, and with much greater advantage than the "justice" which my legal antagonist had praised so highly. But the lawyer replied that such a system could never be practised in England without putting the commonwealth in serious peril. And so saying, he shook his head, made a wry face, and fell silent. And all the company signified their agreement in his opinion.

'Then the Cardinal remarked, "It is not easy to guess whether this scheme would work well or not, since nobody has tried it out. But perhaps when the death sentence has been passed on a thief, the king might reprieve him for a time without right of sanctuary,[36] and thus see how the plan worked. If it turned out well, he might establish it by law; if not, he could execute immediate punishment on the man already condemned. This would be no more perilous to the public or unjust to the criminal than if the condemned man had been put to death at once, yet the experiment would involve no risk. I think vagabonds too might very well be treated this way, for though we have passed laws against them, they have had no real effect as yet."

'When the Cardinal had concluded, they all began praising

---

[36] In earlier days almost any criminal could take sanctuary in any church and be safe from the law. Beginning in the reign of Henry VII, the privilege was gradually abridged. The issue was much disputed in More's time, and is debated in his *Richard III* (*CW*, II, 27–33).

enthusiastically ideas which they had received with contempt when I suggested them; and they particularly liked the idea about vagabonds because it was the Cardinal's addition.

'I don't know whether it's worthwhile telling what followed, because it was silly, but I'll tell it anyhow, for there's no harm in it, and it bears on our subject. There was a parasite standing around, who liked to play the fool, and was so good at it that you could hardly tell him from the real thing. He was constantly making jokes, but so awkwardly that we laughed more at him than at them; yet sometimes a rather clever thing came out, confirming the old proverb that a man who throws the dice often will sooner or later make a lucky cast. One of the company happened to say, "Well, Raphael has taken care of the thieves, and the Cardinal of the vagabonds, so now all we have to do is take care of the poor, whom sickness or old age has kept from earning a living."

'"Leave that to me," said the fool, "and I'll set it right at once. These are people I'm eager to get out of my sight, having been so often vexed with them and their miserable complaints. No matter how pitifully they beg for money, they've never whined a single penny out of my pocket. For they can't win with me: either I don't want to give them anything, or I haven't anything to give them. Now they're getting wise; they know me so well, they don't waste their breath, but let me pass without a word or a hope – no more, by heaven, than if I were a priest. But I would make a law parcelling out all these beggars among the Benedictine monasteries, where the men could become lay brothers, as they're called,[37] and the women could be nuns."

'The Cardinal smiled and passed it off as a joke; the rest took it seriously. But a certain friar, graduate in divinity, found such pleasure in this jest at the expense of priests and monks that he too began to make merry, though generally he was grave to the point of sourness. "You will not get rid of the beggars", he began, "unless you provide for us friars too."

'"You have been taken care of already", retorted the parasite. "The Cardinal provided for you splendidly when he said vagabonds should be arrested and put to work, for you friars are the greatest vagabonds of all."

The friar and the fool: a merry dialogue

A common saying of beggars

---

[37] 'Lay brothers' lived and worked in monasteries (performing mostly menial tasks) but were not admitted to clerical orders.

'When the company, watching the Cardinal closely, saw that he admitted this joke like the other, they all took it up with vigour – except for the friar. Not surprisingly, he was stung by the vinegar and flew into such a rage that he could not keep from abusing the fool. He called him a knave, a slanderer, a sneak and a "son of perdition", quoting the meanwhile terrible denunciations from Holy Writ. Now the joker began to jest in earnest, for he was clearly on his own ground.

A Horatian allusion: 'doused with Italian vinegar' [38]

'"Don't get angry, good friar," he said, "for it is written, *In your patience possess ye your souls.*"[39]

'In reply, the friar said, and I quote his very words: "I am not angry, you gallows-bird, or at least I do not sin, for the Psalmist says, *Be ye angry, and sin not.*"[40]

How his people speak in character!

'At this point the Cardinal gently cautioned the friar to calm down, but he answered, "No, my lord, I speak only from great zeal, as I ought to. For holy men have had great zeal. That is why Scripture says, *The zeal of thine house hath eaten me up,*[41] and we sing in church, *Those who mocked Elisha as he went up to the house of God felt the zeal of the baldhead.*[42] Just so this mocker, this joker, this guttersnipe may well feel it."

Out of ignorance, the friar uses 'zelus' as if it were a neuter noun, like 'scelus' [43]

'"Perhaps you mean well," said the Cardinal, "but I think you would act in a more holy, and certainly in a wiser way, if you didn't set your wit against a fool's wit and try to spar with a professional jester."

'"No, my lord," he replied, "I would not act more wisely. For Solomon himself, wisest of men, said, *Answer a fool according to his folly,*[44] and that's what I'm doing now. I am showing him the pit into which he will fall if he does not take care. For if the many mockers of Elisha, who was only one bald man, felt the zeal of a baldhead, how much more of an effect shall be felt by a single mocker of many

---

[38] *Satires* I.vii.32.

[39] Luke 21:19.

[40] Psalms 4:4. (The Vulgate translates as *Irascimini* ('Be ye angry') the Hebrew word that is rendered 'Stand in awe' in the King James Version.)

[41] Psalms 69:9.

[42] Some children mocked Elisha, son of the prophet Elijah, for his baldness. But his curse brought two bears out of the woods, who tore to pieces forty-two of the mockers: II Kings 2:23–4. The friar quotes a medieval hymn, ascribed to Adam of St Victor, that is based on this cautionary tale.

[43] In the Latin, the friar incorrectly says *zelus* instead of *zelum*.

[44] Proverbs 26:5. The preceding verse, however, says 'Answer not a fool according to his folly, lest thou also be like unto him.'

friars, who include a great many baldheads! And besides, we have a papal bull, by which all who mock at us are excommunicated."

'When the Cardinal saw there was no end to the matter, he nodded to the fool to leave and tactfully turned the conversation to another subject. Soon after, he rose from table and, going to hear petitioners, dismissed us.

'Look, my dear More, what a long story I have inflicted on you. I would be quite ashamed if you had not yourself insisted on it, and seemed to listen as if you did not want any part to be left out. Though I might have shortened my account somewhat, I have recited it in full, so you might see how those who rejected what I said at first approved of it immediately afterwards, when they saw the Cardinal did not disapprove. In fact they went so far in their flattery that they indulged and almost took seriously ideas that he tolerated only as the jesting of a fool. From this episode you can see how little courtiers would value me or my advice.'

To this I answered, 'You have given me great pleasure, my dear Raphael, for everything you've said has been both wise and witty. As you spoke, I seemed to be a child and in my own native land once more, through the pleasant recollection of that Cardinal in whose court I was brought up as a lad. Dear as you are to me on other accounts, you cannot imagine how much dearer you are because you honour his memory so highly. Still, I don't give up my former opinion: I think if you could overcome your aversion to court life, your advice to a prince would be of the greatest advantage to mankind. No part of a good man's duty – and that means yours – is more important than this. Your friend Plato thinks that commonwealths will be happy only when philosophers become kings or kings become philosophers.[45] No wonder we are so far from happiness when philosophers do not condescend even to assist kings with their counsels.'

'They are not so ill disposed', Raphael replied, 'but that they would gladly do it; in fact, many have already done it in published books, if the rulers were only willing to take their good advice. But doubtless Plato was right in foreseeing that unless kings became philosophical themselves, the advice of real philosophers would never influence them, immersed as they are and infected with false values from boyhood on. Plato certainly had this experience with

---

[45] *Republic* V.473C–D; cf. *Epistles* VII.326A–B.

Dionysius of Syracuse.[46] If I proposed wise laws to some king, and tried to root out of his soul the seeds of evil and corruption, don't you suppose I would be either banished forthwith, or treated with scorn?

'Imagine, if you will, that I am at the court of the King of France.[47] Suppose me to be sitting in his royal council, meeting in secret session with the King himself presiding and all his trusty councillors hard at work devising a set of crafty machinations by which the King might keep hold of Milan and recover Naples, which has proved so slippery;[48] then overthrow the Venetians and subdue all Italy; next add to his realm Flanders, Brabant and the whole of Burgundy, besides some other nations he has long had in mind to invade. One man urges him to make an alliance with the Venetians for just as long as it suits the King's convenience – perhaps to develop a common strategy with them, and even allow them a share of the loot, which can be recovered later when things work out according to plan. While one recommends hiring German *Landsknechte*,[49] his neighbour proposes paying the Swiss to stay neutral. A fourth suggests soothing the Emperor's angry pride with a lavish donative of gold.[50] Still another thinks a settlement should be made with the King of Aragon, and that, to cement the peace, he should be allowed to take Navarre, though it doesn't really belong to either France or Spain.[51] Finally, someone suggests snaring the Prince of

Indirectly he discourages the French from seizing Italy

Swiss mercenaries

---

[46] Plato is reported to have made three visits to Syracuse, where he conspicuously failed to reform either the tyrant Dionysius the Elder or his son Dionysius the Younger. See Plato, Epistle VII; Plutarch, 'Dion' IV.1–V.3, IX.1–XX.2.

[47] At the time of writing, Francis I was King of France. At the time of Hythloday's supposed visit to England, the French King was either Charles VIII (d. 1498) or Louis XII (d. 1515). All three were would-be imperialists with hereditary claims to Milan and Naples, and all three bogged down in the intricacies of Italian political intrigue. In general, the advice of the councillors in this passage conforms closely to actual French policies in the period. Rabelais probably had this passage in mind in *Gargantua and Pantagruel* I.xxxiii, where he sketched King Picrochole's insanely tottery schemes of world conquest.

[48] France gained Milan in 1499, lost it in 1512, and regained it at the Battle of Marignano in September 1515. Naples was won in 1495, lost in 1496, won again in 1501, and lost again in 1504.

[49] Among the mercenaries of Europe, the German foot soldiers were surpassed only by the Swiss.

[50] Maximilian of Hapsburg, the Holy Roman Emperor, was notoriously impecunious.

[51] Ferdinand of Aragon took the southern part of Navarre in 1512, and annexed it to Castile (of which he was regent) in 1515.

Castile by the prospect of a marriage alliance: a first step would be to buy up some nobles of his court with secret pensions.[52]

'The hardest problem of all is what to do about England. They all agree that peace should be made, and that the alliance, which is weak at best, should be strengthened as much as possible; but while the English are being proclaimed as friends, they should also be suspected as enemies. And so the Scots must be kept in constant readiness, poised to attack the English in case they stir ever so little.[53] Also a banished nobleman with pretensions to the English throne must be secretly encouraged (treaties forbid doing it openly), and in this way pressure can be applied to the English king, and a ruler kept in check who cannot really be trusted.[54]

'Now in a meeting like this one, where so much is at stake, where so many brilliant men are competing to think up schemes of conquest, what if an insignificant fellow like myself were to get up and advise going on another tack entirely? Suppose I said the King should leave Italy alone and stay at home, because the kingdom of France by itself is almost too much for one man to govern, and the King should not dream of adding others to it?[55] Then imagine I told *A notable example* about the decrees of the Achorians,[56] who live off to the southeast of the island of Utopia. Long ago these people went to war to gain another realm for their king, who had inherited an ancient claim to it through marriage. When they had conquered it, they soon saw that keeping it was going to be no less trouble than getting it had been. Their new subjects were continually rebelling or being attacked by foreign invaders; the Achorians had to be constantly at war for them or against them, and they saw no hope of ever being able to disband their army. In the meantime, they were being heavily

---

[52] Charles, Prince of Castile, was the future Holy Roman Emperor. The question of a French marriage for him, which would unite the two great European powers, was continually in the air. (He was engaged ten different times – always for financial or dynastic reasons – before he was twenty.) On the use of international bribery as an everyday tactic of European statecraft, see James W. Thompson and Saul K. Padover, *Secret Diplomacy*, 2nd edn (New York, 1963), pp. 56–60.

[53] The Scots, as traditional enemies of England, were traditional allies of France.

[54] The French had in fact supported various pretenders to the English throne – most recently, Richard de la Pole, the inheritor of the Yorkist claim.

[55] Cf. More's epigram 'On the Lust for Power': 'Among many kings there will be scarcely one, if there is really one, who is satisfied to have one kingdom. And yet among many kings there will be scarcely one, if there is really one, who rules a single kingdom well' (*CW*, III, Part 2, 257).

[56] From *a-* ('without') plus *xoros* ('place', 'country'): 'the People without a Country'.

taxed, money flowed out of their kingdom, their blood was being shed for someone else's petty pride, and peace was no closer than it had ever been. The war corrupted their citizens by encouraging lust for robbery and murder; and the laws fell into contempt because their king, distracted with the cares of two kingdoms, could give neither his proper attention.

'When they saw that the list of these evils was endless, the Achorians took counsel together, and very courteously offered their king his choice of keeping whichever of the two kingdoms he preferred, because he couldn't rule them both. They were too numerous a people, they said, to be ruled by half a king; adding that a man would not even hire a muledriver if he had to share his services with someone else. The worthy king was thus obliged to be content with his own realm and give his new one to a friend, who before long was driven out.

'Finally, suppose I told the French King's council that all this war-mongering, by which so many different nations were kept in turmoil by one man's connivings, would certainly exhaust his treasury and demoralise his people, yet in the end come to nothing through one mishap or another.[57] And therefore I would advise the king to look after his ancestral kingdom, improve it as much as possible, cultivate it in every conceivable way. He should love his people and be loved by them; he should live among them, govern them kindly, and let other kingdoms alone, since his own is big enough, if not too big, for him. How do you think, my dear More, the other councillors would take this speech of mine?'

'Not very well, I'm sure', said I.

'Well, let's go on', he said. 'Suppose that a king and his councillors are deliberating about various schemes for filling his treasury. One man recommends increasing the value of money when the king pays his debts and devaluing it when he collects his revenues. Thus he can discharge a huge debt with a small payment, and collect a large sum when only a small one is due him.[58] Another

---

[57] Francis lost Milan in 1520 and, in a catastrophic effort to regain it in 1525, was defeated and taken prisoner by Charles V.

[58] Dodges of this kind were practised by Edward IV, Henry VII and (after *Utopia* was written) Henry VIII. In general, the policies satirised in this continuation find more parallels in recent English practice than elsewhere, though European parallels also abound.

suggests a make-believe war, so that money can be raised under pretext of carrying it on; then when the money is in, he can ceremoniously make peace – which the deluded common people will attribute to the prince's piety and compassion for the lives of his subjects.[59] Another councillor calls to mind some old moth-eaten laws, antiquated by long disuse, which no one remembers being made and therefore everyone has transgressed. There's no richer source of supply than fines for breaking these laws, nor any that looks more creditable, since it can be made to wear the mask of justice.[60] Another recommendation is that he forbid under particularly heavy fines many practices, especially such as are contrary to the public interest; afterwards, for large sums of money he can grant the special interests special exemptions from his own rules. Thus he makes a double profit, from fines imposed on those who've fallen into his trap and from selling licenses – the more expensive the better – for other people to be exempt. Meanwhile he pleases the people by seeming solicitous of their welfare and standing up for the public good, which he won't allow anyone to violate except for a huge sum.

'Another councillor proposes that he work on the judges so they will decide every case in the royal interest. They should be frequently summoned to court, and asked to debate his affairs in the royal presence. However unjust his claims, one or another of the judges, whether from love of contradiction, or desire to seem original, or simply to serve his own interest, will be able to find some trick or quibble with which to twist the law in the king's favour. If the judges can be brought to differ, the clearest matter in the world can be made cloudy, and truth itself brought into question. The king is given a convenient handle to interpret the law as he will, and everyone else will acquiesce from shame or fear. Then the judges can boldly pronounce in the royal interest, since pretexts for such a judgement are never in short supply. Either equity is on the king's side, or the letter of the law makes for him, or the words of the law

---

[59] Something like this happened in 1492, when Henry VII not only pretended war with France on behalf of Brittany and levied taxes for the war (which was hardly fought), but collected a bribe from Charles VIII for not fighting it.

[60] Henry VII's ministers Empson and Dudley were notorious masters in this practice – and Cardinal Morton was also involved in it.

can be twisted into obscurity, or else one can invoke the royal prerogative, which in the end outweighs all the laws with judges who know their "duty".[61]

'Then all the councillors agree with the famous maxim of Crassus: a king who must maintain an army can never have too much gold.[62] Further, that a king, even if he wants to, can do no wrong, for all property belongs to the king, and so do his subjects themselves; a man owns nothing but what the king, in his goodness, sees fit to leave him. The king should leave his subjects as little as possible, because his own safety depends on keeping them from growing insolent with wealth and freedom. For riches and liberty make men less patient to endure harsh and unjust commands, whereas meagre poverty blunts their spirits, makes them docile, and grinds out of the oppressed the lofty spirit of rebellion.[63]

Saying of Crassus the Rich

'Now at this point, suppose I were to get up again and declare that all these counsels are both dishonourable and ruinous to the king? Suppose I said his honour and his safety alike rest on the people's resources, rather than his own? Suppose I said that men choose a king for their own sake, not his, so that by his efforts and troubles they may live in comfort and safety? This is why, I would say, it is the king's duty to take more care of his people's welfare than of his own,

---

[61] The limits of royal prerogative, and the duties of judges (who served by royal appointment) in respect to it, was in the course of becoming an issue of the utmost importance. For an overview, see John W. Allen, *A History of Political Thought in the Sixteenth Century* (1928; rpt, London, 1957), pp. 121–68.

[62] Hythloday adapts his source, which is Cicero's *On Moral Obligation*: 'Crassus ... not long since declared that no amount of wealth was enough for the man who aspired to be the foremost citizen of the state, unless with the income from it he could maintain an army' (I.viii.25). Crassus joined with Pompey and Caesar to form the First Triumvirate (60 BC).

[63] The underlying schema of the foregoing paragraphs was provided by Aristotle's discussion in the *Politics* of the two ways in which tyrannies can be preserved. The first embraces the traditional acts of the tyrant: he will prohibit 'everything likely to produce ... mutual confidence and a high spirit' in the citizens (v.xi.5); his 'first end and aim is to break the spirit of ... [his] subjects', because 'a poor-spirited man will never plot against anybody' (xi.15). Impoverishing the citizens is a principal means to this end. Alternatively, 'the tyrant should act, or at any rate appear to act, in the role of a good player of the part of King' (xi.19). He should, for example, 'levy taxes, and require other contributions, in such a way that they can be seen to be intended for the proper management of public services, or to be meant for use ... on military emergencies' (xi.21).

just as it is the duty of a shepherd who cares about his job to feed the sheep rather than himself.[64]

'They are absolutely wrong when they say the people's poverty guarantees public peace: experience shows the contrary. Where will you find more squabbling than among beggars? Who is more eager for revolution than the man who is most discontented with his present position? Who is more reckless about creating disorder than the man who knows he has nothing to lose and thinks he may have something to gain? If a king is so hated or despised by his subjects that he can rule them only by maltreatment, plundering, confiscation and pauperisation, he'd do much better to abdicate his throne – for under these circumstances, though he keeps the name of authority, he loses all the majesty of a king. A king has no dignity when he exercises authority over beggars, only when he rules over prosperous and happy subjects. This was certainly what that noble and lofty spirit Fabricius meant, when he said he would rather be a ruler of rich men than be rich himself.[65]

'A solitary ruler who enjoys a life of pleasure and self-indulgence while all about him are grieving and groaning is acting like a jailer, not a king. Just as an incompetent doctor can cure his patient of one disease only by throwing him into another, so it's an incompetent monarch who can reform his people only by depriving them of all life's pleasures. Such a king openly confesses his incapacity to rule free men.

'A king of this stamp should correct his own sloth or arrogance, because these are the vices that cause people to hate or despise him. Let him live on his own income without wronging others, and limit his spending to his income. Let him curb crime, and by training his subjects wisely keep them from misbehaviour, instead of letting trouble breed and then punishing it. Let him not suddenly revive antiquated laws, especially if they have been long forgotten and never missed. And let him never take money as a fine when a judge would regard an ordinary subject as a low fraud for claiming it.

'Suppose I should then describe for them the law of the

---

[64] Again Hythloday's advice is the same as that offered by More speaking in his own person (e.g., *Epigrams*, *CW*, III, Part 2, 163–5, 169).

[65] Gaius Fabricius Luscinus took part in the wars against Pyrrhus, King of Epirus (280–275 BC). The saying that is attributed to him here was actually coined by his colleague Manius Curius Dentatus (Plutarch, *Moral Essays* 194F), but it is quite in his spirit.

Macarians,[66] a people who also live not far from the Utopians. On the day that their king first assumes office, he must swear a solemn oath never to have in his treasury at any one time more than a thousand pounds of gold, or its equivalent in silver.[67] They say this law was made by an excellent king, who cared more for his country's welfare than for his own wealth, and wanted to prevent any king from heaping up so much money as to impoverish his people. He thought this sum would enable the king to put down rebellions or repel hostile invasions, but would not tempt him into aggressive adventures. Though his law was aimed chiefly at checking the monarch, he also wanted to ensure an ample supply of money for the daily business of the citizens. Finally, a king who has to distribute all his excess money to the people will not be much disposed to oppress them. Such a king will be feared by evil-doers, and just as much beloved by the good. – Now, don't you suppose if I set these ideas and others like them before men strongly inclined to the contrary, they would "turn deaf ears" to me?'

Wonderful law of the Macarians

Proverb

'Stone deaf, indeed, there's no doubt about it,' I said, 'and no wonder! To tell you the truth, I don't think you should offer advice or thrust forward ideas of this sort that you know will not be listened to. What good will it do? When your listeners are already prepossessed against you and firmly convinced of opposite opinions, what can you accomplish with your out-of-the-way notions? This academic philosophy is pleasant enough in the private conversation of close friends, but in the councils of kings, where grave matters are being authoritatively decided, there is no room for it.'[68]

'That is just what I was saying', Raphael replied. 'There is no place for philosophy in the councils of kings.'

'Yes, there is,' I said, 'but not for this school philosophy which supposes that every topic is suitable for every occasion.[69] There is

Philosophy of the Schools

---

[66] From *makarios*: 'blessed', 'happy'.

[67] Again More seems to glance at Henry VII, who died with a huge sum in his treasury.

[68] This position is informed by the rhetorical and ethical doctrine of *decorum*, propriety of words or actions. (On *decorum*, see Cicero, *Orator* XXII.74, *On Moral Obligation* I. xxvii–xlii.) The ensuing argument reflects the ancient conflict between rhetoric and philosophy, which centres in the tension between persuasion and truth.

[69] Complaints that scholastic philosophers fail to consider context – whether in the interpretation of literary works or in their mistaken notions about style and rhetorical strategy – constitute a main theme of humanist attacks on scholasticism. See, for example, More's 'Letter to Dorp', *Selected Letters*, pp. 29–32. So More's speech is a real insult to Hythloday.

another philosophy, better suited for the political arena, that takes its cue, adapts itself to the drama in hand, and acts its part neatly and appropriately. This is the philosophy for you to use.[70] When a comedy of Plautus is being played, and the household slaves are cracking trivial jokes together, you propose to come on stage in the garb of a philosopher, and repeat Seneca's speech to Nero from the *Octavia*.[71] Wouldn't it be better to take a silent role than to say something wholly inappropriate, and thus turn the play into a tragicomedy? You pervert a play and ruin it when you add irrelevant speeches, even if they are better than the play itself. So go through with the drama in hand as best you can, and don't spoil it all just because you happen to think of another one that would be better.

A striking comparison

A mute part

'That's how things go in the commonwealth, and in the councils of princes. If you cannot pluck up bad ideas by the root, or cure long-standing evils to your heart's content, you must not therefore abandon the commonwealth. Don't give up the ship in a storm because you cannot direct the winds. And don't force strange and untested ideas on people who you know are firmly persuaded the other way. You must strive to influence policy indirectly, urge your case vigorously but tactfully, and thus what you cannot turn to good, you may at least make as little bad as possible.[72] For it is impossible to make everything good unless all men are good, and that I don't expect to see for quite a few years yet.'

'The only result of this', he answered, 'will be that while I try to cure others of madness, I'll be raving along with them myself. If I'm to speak the truth, I will have to talk in the way I've described. Whether it's the business of a philosopher to tell lies, I don't know, but it isn't mine. Perhaps my advice may be repugnant to the king's councillors, but I don't see why they should consider it eccentric to the point of folly. What if I told them the kind of thing that Plato sketches in his *Republic*, or that the Utopians actually practise in theirs? However superior those institutions might be (and they

Utopian institutions

[70] Cf. Cicero, *Orator* XXXV.123: 'This ... is the form of wisdom that the orator must especially employ – to adapt himself to occasions and persons ... one must not speak in the same style at all times, nor before all people.'

[71] Most of the plays of the Roman comic dramatist Plautus involve low intrigue: needy young men, expensive prostitutes, senile moneybags, and clever slaves, in predictable combinations. The tragedy *Octavia*, involving Seneca as a character, but not by him (though long supposed to be so), is full of high seriousness.

[72] This is consistent with the advice of rhetoricians (e.g., Quintilian, *The Education of the Orator* II.xvii.26–9, III.viii.38–9).

certainly are), yet here they would seem inappropriate because private property is the rule here and there all things are held in common.

'People who have made up their minds to rush headlong down the opposite road are never pleased with the man who calls them back and points out the dangers of their course. But, apart from that, what did I say that could not and should not be said everywhere? If we dismiss as out of the question and absurd everything that the perverse customs of men have made to seem unusual, we shall have to set aside, even in a community of Christians, most of the commandments of Christ. Yet he forbade us to dissemble them, and even ordered that what he had whispered in the ears of his disciples should be preached openly from the housetops.[73] Most of his teachings differ far more radically from the common customs of mankind than my discourse did. But preachers, like the crafty fellows they are, have found that men would rather not change their lives to fit Christ's rule, and so, just as you suggest, they have adjusted his teaching to the way men live, as if it were a leaden yardstick.[74] At least in that way they can get the two things to correspond on one level or another. The only real thing they accomplish that I can see is to make men feel more secure in their consciences about doing evil.

'And this is all that I could accomplish in the councils of princes. For either I would have different ideas from the others, and that would be like having no ideas at all, or I would agree with them, and that, as Mitio says in Terence, would merely confirm them in their madness.[75] When you say I should "influence policy indirectly", I simply don't know what you mean; remember, you said I should try hard to urge my case tactfully, and what can't be made good I should try to make as little bad as possible. In a council, there is no way to dissemble or play the innocent. You must openly approve the worst proposals and warmly urge the most vicious policies. A man who went along only half-heartedly would immediately be suspected as a spy, perhaps a traitor. How can one individual do any good when he

---

[73] Matthew 10:27; Luke 12:3.

[74] A flexible measuring rod of lead was particularly useful in the sort of ancient building known as the 'Lesbian' style, because of the great number of curved mouldings. Aristotle uses the leaden rod as a metaphor for adaptable moral standards (*Nicomachean Ethics* v.x.7).

[75] The allusion is to a comedy – *The Brothers* (1.145–7) – by the Roman playwright Terence.

is surrounded by colleagues who would more readily corrupt the best of men than be reformed themselves? Either they will seduce you, or, if you remain honest and innocent, you will be made a screen for the knavery and folly of others. Influencing policy indirectly! You wouldn't have a chance.

'This is why Plato in a very fine comparison[76] declares that wise men are right in keeping away from public business. They see the people swarming through the streets and getting soaked with rain; they cannot persuade them to go indoors and get out of the wet. If they go out themselves, they know they will do no good, but only get drenched with the others. So they stay indoors and are content to keep themselves dry, since they cannot remedy the folly of everyone else.

'But as a matter of fact, my dear More, to tell you what I really think, wherever you have private property, and money is the measure of all things, it is hardly ever possible for a commonwealth to be governed justly or happily – unless you think justice can exist where all the best things in life are held by the worst citizens, or suppose happiness can be found where property is limited to a few – where even those few are always uneasy, and where the many are utterly wretched.

'So I reflect on the wonderfully wise and sacred institutions of the Utopians, who are so well governed with so few laws.[77] Among them virtue has its reward, yet everything is shared equally, and all men live in plenty. I contrast with them the many other nations, none of which, though all are constantly passing new ordinances, can ever order its affairs satisfactorily. In these other nations, whatever a man can get he calls his own private property; but all the mass of laws old and new don't enable him to secure his own, to defend it, or even to distinguish it from someone else's property. Different men lay claim, successively or all at once, to the same property; and thus arise innumerable and interminable lawsuits, fresh ones every day. When I consider all these things, I become more sympathetic to Plato, and wonder the less that he refused to make laws for any people who would not share their goods equally. Wisest of men, he saw easily that the one and only path to the welfare of all lies through

---

[76] *Republic* VI.496D–E.

[77] On the small number of Utopian laws (though they are supplemented by an oppressive number of codes, customs and conventions), see p. 84.

equality of possessions.[78] I doubt whether such equality can ever be achieved where property belongs to individual men. However abundant goods may be, when every man tries to get as much as he can for his own exclusive use, a handful of men end up sharing the whole pile, and the rest are left in poverty. The result generally is two sorts of people whose fortunes ought to be interchanged: the rich are rapacious, wicked and useless, while the poor are unassuming, modest men, who work hard more for the benefit of the public than of themselves.

'Thus I am wholly convinced that unless private property is entirely abolished, there can be no fair or just distribution of goods, nor can mankind be happily governed. As long as private property remains, by far the largest and best part of mankind will be oppressed by a heavy and inescapable burden of poverty and anxieties. This load, I admit, may be partly lightened under the present system, but I maintain it cannot be entirely removed. Laws might be made that no one should own more than a certain amount of land or receive more than a certain income. Or laws might be passed to prevent the prince from becoming too powerful and the populace too unruly. It might be made illegal for public offices to be solicited or put up for sale or made burdensome for the office-holder by great expense. Otherwise, officials are tempted to get their money back by fraud or extortion, and only rich men can accept appointment to positions which ought to go to the wise. Laws of this sort, I agree, may have as much effect as good and careful nursing has on persons who are chronically sick. The social evils I mentioned may be alleviated and their effects mitigated for a while, but so long as private property remains, there is no hope at all of effecting a cure and restoring society to good health. While you try to cure one part, you aggravate the disease in other parts. Suppressing one symptom causes another to

---

[78] Diogenes Laertius reports that 'the Arcadians and Thebans, when they were founding Megalopolis, invited Plato to be their legislator; but . . . when he discovered that they were opposed to equality of possessions, he refused to go' (*Lives of Eminent Philosophers* III.23). But in the *Republic* Plato recommends communism only for the ruling class (the Guardians). Given its approval by Plato, Plutarch and, traditionally, Pythagoras, as well as the stress in the New Testament on the communal life of the earliest Christians, communism had long been respectable as an intellectual position. The first proverb discussed in Erasmus' *Adages* is *Amicorum communia omnia* ('Between friends all is common'), and Erasmus remarks that 'it is extraordinary how Christians dislike this common ownership of Plato's, . . . although nothing was ever said by a pagan philosopher which comes closer to the mind of Christ' (*CWE*, XXXI, 30).

break out, since you cannot give something to one man without taking it away from someone else.'

'But I don't see it that way', I replied. 'It seems to me that men cannot possibly live well where all things are in common. How can there be plenty of commodities where every man stops working? If the hope of gain does not spur him on, won't he rely on others, and become lazy? If men are impelled by need, and yet no man can legally protect what he has obtained, what can follow but continual bloodshed and turmoil, especially when respect for magistrates and their authority has been lost? I for one cannot conceive of authority existing among men who are equal to one another in every respect.'[79]

'I'm not surprised that you think of it this way,' said Raphael, 'since you have no idea or only a false idea of such a commonwealth. But you should have been with me in Utopia and seen with your own eyes their manners and customs, as I did – for I lived there more than five years, and would never have left, if it had not been to make that new world known to others. If you had seen them, you would frankly confess that you had never seen a well-governed people anywhere but there.'

'Come now,' said Peter Giles, 'you will have a hard time persuading me that people in that new land are better governed than in the world we know. Our minds are not inferior to theirs, and our governments, I believe, are older. Long experience has helped us develop many conveniences of life, and by good luck we have discovered many others that human ingenuity could never hit on.'

'As for the relative ages of the governments,' Raphael replied, 'you might judge more accurately if you had read their histories. If we believe these records, they had cities there before there were even men here. What ingenuity has discovered or chance hit upon could have turned up just as well there as here. For the rest, I really think that even if we surpass them in natural intelligence, they leave us far behind in their diligence and zeal to learn.

'According to their chronicles, they had heard nothing of men-from-beyond-the-equator (that's their name for us) until we arrived, except that once, some twelve hundred years ago, a ship

---

[79] These objections to communism derive from the critique of the *Republic* in Aristotle's *Politics* (II.i–v).

which a storm had blown towards Utopia was wrecked on their island. Some Romans and Egyptians were cast ashore, and never departed.

'Now note how the Utopians profited, through their diligence, from this one chance event. They learned every single useful art of the Roman civilisation either directly from their guests or indirectly from hints and surmises on which they based their own investigations. What benefits from the mere fact that on a single occasion some Europeans landed there! If in the past a similar accident has brought any men here from their land, the incident has been completely forgotten, as our future generations will perhaps forget that I was ever there. From one such accident they made themselves masters of all our useful inventions, but I suspect it will be a long time before we adopt any institutions of theirs which are better than ours. This readiness to learn is, I think, the really important reason for their being better governed and living more happily than we do, though we are not inferior to them in brains or resources.'

'Then let me implore you, my dear Raphael,' said I, 'describe that island to us. Don't try to be brief, but explain in order everything relating to their land, their rivers, towns, people, manners, institutions, laws – everything, in short, that you think we would like to know. And you can assume we want to know everything we don't know yet.'

'There's nothing I'd rather do,' he replied, 'for these things are fresh in my mind. But it will take quite some time.'

'In that case,' I said, 'let's first go to luncheon. Afterwards, we shall have all the time we want.'

'Agreed', he said. So we went in and had lunch. Then we came back to the same spot, and sat down on the bench. I ordered my servants to make sure that no one interrupted us. Peter Giles and I urged Raphael to fulfil his promise. When he saw that we were eager to hear him, he sat silent and thoughtful a moment, and then began as follows.

THE END OF BOOK I

BOOK TWO FOLLOWS

THE DISCOURSE OF RAPHAEL HYTHLODAY
ON THE BEST STATE OF A COMMONWEALTH,
BOOK TWO: AS RECOUNTED BY THOMAS MORE,
CITIZEN AND SHERIFF OF LONDON

Site and shape of Utopia the new island

The island of Utopia is two hundred miles across in the middle part where it is widest, and nowhere much narrower than this except towards the two ends, where it gradually tapers. These ends, curved round as if completing a circle five hundred miles in circumference, make the island crescent-shaped, like a new moon.[1] Between the horns of the crescent, which are about eleven miles apart, the sea enters and spreads into a broad bay. Being sheltered from the wind by the surrounding land, the bay is not rough, but placid and smooth instead, like a big lake. Thus, nearly the whole inner coast is one great harbour, across which ships pass in every direction, to the great advantage of the people. What with shallows on one side, and rocks on the other, entrance into the bay is very dangerous. Near

Being naturally safe, the entry is defended by a single fort

mid-channel, there is one rock that rises above the water, and so presents no danger in itself; a tower has been built on top of it, and a garrison is kept there. Since the other rocks lie under the water, they are very dangerous to navigation. The channels are known only to the Utopians, so hardly any strangers enter the bay without one of their pilots; and even they themselves could not enter safely if they

The trick of shifting landmarks

did not direct their course by some landmarks on the coast. Should these landmarks be shifted about, the Utopians could lure to destruction an enemy fleet coming against them, however big it was.

---

[1] Utopia is similar to England in size, though not at all in shape. For a detailed account of its geography, and the inconsistencies thereof, see Brian R. Goodey, 'Mapping "Utopia": A Comment on the Geography of Sir Thomas More', *The Geographical Review*, 60 (1970), 15–30.

The main topics and the order of Hythloday's account may owe something to Aristotle's treatment of the ideal commonwealth in *Politics* VII–VIII. Aristotle's discussion of the optimal 'human material' and territory for a polis is followed by a checklist of the six 'services' that must be provided for: food; arts and crafts; arms; 'a certain supply of property, alike for domestic use and for military purposes'; public worship; and a deliberative and judicial system (VII.iv–viii).

On the outer side of the island, occasional harbours are to be found; but the coast is rugged by nature, and so well fortified that a few defenders could beat off the attack of a strong force. They say (and the appearance of the place confirms this) that their land was not always an island. But Utopus, who conquered the country and gave it his name (for it had previously been called Abraxa),[2] and who brought its rude, uncouth inhabitants to such a high level of culture and humanity that they now excel in that regard almost every other people, also changed its geography. After subduing the natives, at his first landing, he promptly cut a channel fifteen miles wide where their land joined the continent, and thus caused the sea to flow around the country. He put not only the natives to work at this task, but all his own soldiers too, so that the vanquished would not think the labour a disgrace.[4] With the work divided among so many hands, the project was finished quickly, and the neighbouring peoples, who at first had laughed at his folly, were struck with wonder and terror at his success.

There are fifty-four cities[5] on the island, all spacious and magnificent, identical in language, customs, institutions and laws. So

Utopia named for King Utopus

This was a bigger job than digging across the Isthmus[3]

Many hands make light work

The towns of Utopia

---

[2] The Greek Gnostic Basilides (second century) postulated 365 heavens, and gave the name 'Abraxas' to the highest of them. The Greek letters that constitute the term have numerical equivalents summing to 365, but what 'Abraxas' actually means nobody knows.

[3] The Isthmus of Corinth joins the Peloponnesian peninsula to the rest of Greece. The failure of various attempts to excavate a canal across it made this difficult task proverbial.

[4] This is the first of several passages in *Utopia* stressing the dignity of labour. Frank and Fritzie Manuel observe that 'More's rehabilitation of the idea of physical labor was a milestone in the history of utopian thought, and was incorporated into all socialist systems' (*Utopian Thought in the Western World*, p. 127). The principal sources of this attitude are Christian; in particular, the monastic orders constituted a paradigm of a society in which all are workers. Monasticism is the one European institution that the Utopians are said to admire (p. 96). By contrast, in classical political theory and practice manual labour was normally assigned to members of the lower orders (including especially slaves), and to women.

[5] Although the primary reference here is to the cities themselves, the word More uses – *civitas* – is the Latin equivalent of the Greek *polis*, 'city-state'. In fact each of the fifty-four Utopian *civitates* is, like the Greek *polis*, constituted of a central city and its surrounding countryside. Though federated, they also resemble the Greek city-states in functioning as largely independent political units. Throughout Book II, the concentration on the *civitas* is the most striking indication of More's debt to Greek political theory. In number, the Utopian cities match the number of counties in England and Wales – given as fifty-three in William Harrison's 1587 *Description of England* (ed. Georges Edelen (Ithaca, 1968), p. 86) – plus London.

Likeness breeds concord

far as the location permits, all of them are built on the same plan and have the same appearance. The nearest are at least twenty-four miles apart, and the farthest are not so remote that a man cannot go on foot from one to the other in a day.

A middling distance between towns

Once a year each city sends three of its old and experienced citizens to Amaurot[6] to consider affairs of common interest to the island. Amaurot lies at the navel of the land, so to speak, and convenient to every other district, so it acts as a capital. Every city has enough ground assigned to it so that at least twelve miles of farm land are available in every direction, though where the cities are farther apart, their territories are more extensive. No city wants to enlarge its boundaries, for the inhabitants consider themselves good cultivators rather than landlords. At proper intervals all over the countryside they have built houses and furnished them with farm equipment. These houses are inhabited by citizens who come to the country by turns to occupy them. No rural household has fewer than forty men and women in it, besides two slaves bound to the land. A master and mistress, serious and mature persons, are in charge of each household, and over every thirty households is placed a single phylarch.[8] Each year twenty persons from each rural household move back to the city after completing a two-year stint in the country. In their place, twenty others are sent out from town, to learn farm work from those who have already been in the country for a year, and who are better skilled in farming. They, in turn, will teach those who come the following year. If all were equally untrained in farm work and new to it, they might harm the crops out of ignorance. This custom of alternating farm workers is solemnly established so that no one will have to perform such heavy labour for more than two years; but many of them who take a natural pleasure in farm life are allowed to stay longer.

Distribution of land

But today this is the curse of all countries[7]

Farming is the prime occupation

Farmers' jobs

The farm workers till the soil, feed the animals, hew wood and take their produce to the city by land or water, as is convenient. They breed an enormous number of chickens by a most marvellous method. Men, not hens, hatch the eggs by keeping them in a warm

A notable way of hatching eggs

---

[6] From *amauroton*, 'made dark or dim'.

[7] Although Utopia exists in the present, the glosses repeatedly refer to it as if it belonged to the distant past, like classical Greece and Rome.

[8] Greek *phylarchos*, 'head of a tribe'.

place at an even temperature.[9] As soon as they come out of the shell, the chicks recognise the men, follow them around, and are devoted to them instead of to their real mothers.

They raise very few horses, and these full of mettle, which they keep only to exercise the young men in the art of horsemanship. For the heavy work of ploughing and hauling they use oxen, which they agree are inferior to horses over the short haul, but which can hold out longer under heavy burdens, are less subject to disease (as they suppose), and besides can be kept with less cost and trouble. Moreover, when oxen are too old for work, they can be used for meat.

Uses of the horse

Uses of oxen

Grain they use only to make bread.[10] They drink wine made of grapes, apple or pear cider, or simple water, which they sometimes mix with honey or liquorice, of which they have plenty. Although they know very well, down to the last detail, how much food each city and its surrounding district will consume, they produce much more grain and cattle than they need for themselves, and share the surplus with their neighbours. Whatever goods the folk in the country need which cannot be produced there, they request of the town magistrates, and since there is nothing to be paid or exchanged, they get what they want at once without any haggling. They generally go to town once a month in any case, to observe the holy days. When harvest time approaches, the phylarchs in the country notify the town magistrates how many hands will be needed. Crews of harvesters come just when they're wanted, and in about one day of good weather they can get in the whole crop.

Food and drink

Planned planting

The value of collective labour

THEIR CITIES, ESPECIALLY AMAUROT

If you know one of their cities, you know them all, for they're exactly alike, except where geography itself makes a difference. So I'll describe one of them, and no matter which. But what one rather than Amaurot, the most worthy of all? – since its eminence is acknowledged by the other cities that send representatives to the annual meeting there; besides which, I know it best because I lived there for five full years.

Description of Amaurot, first city of Utopia

Well, then, Amaurot lies up against a gently sloping hill; the town

---

[9] Though artificial incubation is mentioned in Pliny's *Natural History* (x.lxxvi.154), it was not practised in More's time.

[10] I.e., they don't, like the English, use it to make beer and ale.

is almost square in shape. From a little below the crest of the hill, it runs down about two miles to the river Anyder,[11] and then spreads out along the river bank for a somewhat greater distance. The Anyder rises from a small spring eighty miles above Amaurot, but other streams flow into it, two of them being pretty big, so that as it runs by Amaurot the river has grown to a width of about half a mile. It continues to grow even larger until at last, sixty miles farther along, it is lost in the ocean. In all this stretch between the sea and the city, and also for some miles above the city, the river is tidal, ebbing and flowing every six hours with a swift current. When the tide comes in, it fills the whole Anyder with salt water for about thirty miles, driving the fresh water back. Even above that, for several miles farther, the water is brackish; but a little higher up, as it runs past the city, the water is always fresh, and when the tide ebbs, the river runs fresh and clean nearly all the way to the sea.

The river Anyder

Just like the Thames in England

The two banks of the river at Amaurot are linked by a bridge, built not on wooden piles but on massive stone arches. It is placed at the upper end of the city farthest removed from the sea, so that ships can sail along the entire length of the city quays without obstruction.[12] There is also another stream, not particularly large but very gentle and pleasant, that rises out of the hill, flows down through the centre of town, and into the Anyder.[13] The inhabitants have walled around the source of this river, which is a spring somewhat outside the city, and joined it to the town proper, so that if they should be attacked, the enemy would not be able to cut off and divert the stream, or poison it. Water from the stream is carried by tile piping into various sections of the lower town. Where the terrain makes this impractical, they collect rain water in cisterns, which serve just as well.

Here too London is just like Amaurot

A source of drinking water

The town is surrounded by a thick, high wall, with many towers and battlements. On three sides it is also surrounded by a dry ditch, broad and deep and filled with thorn hedges; on its fourth side the river itself serves as a moat. The streets are conveniently laid out for use by vehicles and for protection from the wind. Their buildings

City walls

Streets, of what sort

[11] From *anydros*, 'waterless'. The description of the Anyder and the situation of Amaurot correspond in detail to the Thames and London, except that the Thames rises about twice as far above London as the Anyder above Amaurot.
[12] This is an improvement on the situation of London Bridge, which was in the lower part of town.
[13] Except in pleasantness, this second stream resembles London's Fleet.

are by no means paltry; the unbroken rows of houses facing one *Buildings* another across the streets through each ward make a fine sight. The streets are twenty feet wide.[14] Large gardens, which extend the full *Gardens next to* length of the street behind each row of houses, form the centre of the *the houses* blocks.

Every house has a front door to the street and a back door to the garden. The doors, which are made with two leaves, open easily and swing shut automatically – and so there is nothing private or exclu- *This smacks of* sive.[15] Every ten years they exchange the houses themselves by lot. *Plato's* The Utopians are very fond of these gardens of theirs.[16] They raise *community* vines, fruits, herbs and flowers, so thrifty and flourishing that I have never seen any gardens more productive or elegant than theirs. They keep interested in gardening, partly because they delight in it, and also because of the competition between different neighbour-hoods, which challenge one another to produce the best gardens. Certainly you will find nothing else in the whole city more useful or *Virgil also wrote* more pleasant to the citizens. And from that fact it appears that the *in praise of* city's founder must have made gardens the primary object of his *gardens*[17] consideration.

They say that in the beginning the whole city was planned by King Utopus himself, but that he left to posterity matters of adorn-ment and improvement such as could not be perfected in one man's lifetime. Their records began 1,760 years ago[18] with the conquest of

---

[14] Lavish, by sixteenth-century standards. Goodey observes that the structure of Amaurot is reminiscent of Roman urban planning: 'Twenty feet was the average width of Roman city streets, which, again like Amaurotum, were bordered by fairly high-density housing blocks that surrounded large courtyards used for recreation. As in Amaurotum, the rectangular block pattern was the most evident feature of the Roman urban plan. In the Roman city this pattern was broken only by the insertion of major public buildings, again a feature of the Utopian city' ('Mapping "Utopia"', p. 29).

[15] Cf. Plato, *Republic* v.416D: the Guardians 'shall have no private property beyond the barest essentials ... none of them shall possess a dwelling-house or other property to which all have not the right of entry.'

[16] Apart from its obvious practical advantages, the Utopians' fondness for gardens may hint at the connection of their way of life with Epicureanism. Early in life, Epicurus retired to a house and garden given him by his disciples; and his school was called the Garden.

[17] In the *Georgics* (IV.116–48).

[18] Counting from 1516, this takes us back to 244 BC, when Agis IV became King of Sparta: he was put to death for proposing egalitarian reforms. See Plutarch's 'Agis'; and R. J. Schoeck, 'More, Plutarch, and King Agis: Spartan History and the Meaning of *Uto-pia*', *Philological Quarterly*, 35 (1956), 366–75; rpt *Essential Articles for the Study of Thomas More*.

the island, were diligently compiled, and are carefully preserved in writing. From these records it appears that the first houses were low, like cabins or peasant huts, built slapdash out of any sort of lumber, with mud-plastered walls and steep roofs, ridged and thatched with straw. But now their houses are all three storeys high and handsomely constructed; the fronts are faced with stone, stucco, or brick, over rubble construction.[19] The roofs are flat and are covered with a kind of plaster that is cheap but fireproof, and more weather-resistant even than lead.[20] Glass (of which they have a good supply) is used in windows to keep out the weather; and they also use thin linen cloth treated with clear oil or gum so that it lets in more light and keeps out more wind.

Windows of glass or oiled linen

THEIR OFFICIALS

Once a year, every group of thirty households elects an official, called the syphogrant in their ancient language,[21] but now known as the phylarch. Over every group of ten syphogrants with their households there is another official, once called the tranibor but

In the Utopian tongue 'tranibor' means 'chief official'

---

[19] The housing of modern Amaurot is considerably more impressive than that of early sixteenth-century London, where dwellings were normally of timber and of at most two storeys.

[20] The Utopians' roof-covering may be the plaster of Paris spoken of in Harrison's *Description of England*, which was made of 'fine alabaster burned, ... whereof in some places we have great plenty and that very profitable against the rage of fire' (p. 196). Glass windows were uncommon in England. Oiled linen, sheets of horn, and lattices of wicker or wood were used instead.

[21] 'Syphogrant' appears to be constructed from Greek *sophos* ('wise') – or perhaps *sypheos* ('of the sty') – plus *gerontes* ('old men'). For 'tranibor', the obvious etymology is *traneis* or *tranos* ('clear', 'plain', 'distinct') plus *boros* ('devouring', 'gluttonous'). Although Hythloday says that these terms have been displaced by the more unambiguously respectful 'phylarch' and 'protophylarch' (translated as 'head phylarch'), in the remainder of his account he invariably uses the 'older' terms. 'Phylarch' occurs twice before this passage, but never again; 'protophylarch' occurs only this once.

The Utopian form of government is republican: syphogrants are elected by the households, and the syphogrants of each city elect – and can remove – the prince (below), as well as the class of scholars, from which all high officials are chosen (p. 53). On the revival of classical republican sentiment in the Renaissance, see Hans Baron, *The Crisis of the Early Italian Renaissance*, rev. one-vol. edn (Princeton, 1966); J. G. A. Pocock, *The Machiavellian Moment: Florentine Political Thought and the Atlantic Republican Tradition* (Princeton, 1975); and Quentin Skinner, *The Foundations of Modern Political Thought*.

now known as the head phylarch. All the syphogrants, two hundred in number,[22] are brought together to elect the prince. They take an oath to choose the man they think best qualified; and then by secret ballot they elect the prince from among four men nominated by the people of the four sections of the city.[23] The prince holds office for life, unless he is suspected of aiming at a tyranny. Though the tranibors are elected annually, they are not changed for light or casual reasons. All their other officials hold office for a single year only.

A notable way of electing officials

Tyranny hateful to the well-ordered commonwealth

The tranibors meet to consult with the prince every other day, more often if necessary: they discuss affairs of state and settle disputes between private parties (if there are any, and there are very few), acting as quickly as possible. The tranibors always invite two syphogrants to the senate chamber, different ones every day. There is a rule that no decision can be made on a matter of public business unless it has been discussed in the senate on three separate days. It is a capital offence to join in reaching private decisions on public business.[24] The purpose of these rules, they say, is to prevent prince and tranibors from conspiring together to alter the government and enslave the people. Therefore all matters which are considered important are first laid before the assembly of syphogrants. They talk the matter over with the households they represent, debate it with one another, then report their recommendation to the senate. Sometimes a question is brought before the general council of the whole island.

A quick ending to disputes, which now are endlessly and deliberately prolonged

No abrupt decisions

The senate also has a standing rule never to debate a matter on the same day that it is first introduced; all new business is deferred to the next meeting. This they do so that a man will not blurt out the first thought that occurs to him, and then devote all his energies to defending his own prestige, instead of impartially considering the common interest. They know that some men have such a perverse and preposterous sense of shame that they would rather jeopardise the general welfare than admit to having been heedless and short-

Would that the same rules prevailed in our modern councils

This is the old saying, 'Do your thinking overnight'

---

[22] Because there are 6,000 families in each city (p. 55), with thirty families per syphogrant.

[23] While each city has a prince, there is no prince over the whole island, so that when the national council meets at Amaurot (p. 44) there's nobody for it to advise – no executive.

[24] The remainder of the paragraph suggests that the purpose of this rule – which our translation, like More's Latin, leaves ambiguous – is to discourage conspiracies rather than to inhibit all private discussion of politics.

sighted. They should have had enough foresight at the beginning to speak with prudence rather than haste.

THEIR OCCUPATIONS

Agriculture is everyone's business, though now we put it off on a despised few

Farming is the one job at which everyone works, men and women alike, with no exception.[25] They are trained in it from childhood, partly in the schools, where they learn theory, partly through field trips to nearby farms, which make something like a game of practical instruction. On these trips they not only watch the work being done, but frequently pitch in and get a workout by doing the jobs themselves.

Trades taught to satisfy need, not greed

A uniform dress code

Besides farm work (which, as I said, everybody performs), each person is taught a particular trade of his own, such as wool-working, linen-making, masonry, metal-work, or carpentry. There is no other craft that is practised by any considerable number of them.[26] Their clothing – which is the same everywhere throughout the island, and has always been the same, except for the distinction between the sexes and between married and unmarried persons – which is by no means unattractive, does not hinder bodily movement and serves for warm as well as cold weather – this clothing, I say, each family makes for itself.

No citizen without a trade

Everyone to learn the trade for which his nature fits him

Every person (and this includes women as well as men) learns one of the trades I mentioned. As the weaker sex, women practise the lighter crafts, such as working in wool or linen; the heavier jobs are assigned to the men. Ordinarily, the son is trained to his father's craft, for which most feel a natural inclination. But if anyone is attracted to another occupation, he is transferred by adoption into a family practising the trade he prefers. When anyone makes such a change, both his father and the authorities take care that he is assigned to a grave and responsible householder. After a man has mastered one trade, if he wants to learn another, he gets the same

[25] Agriculture gets the same heavy emphasis in *Utopia* as it did in sixteenth-century Europe, where most of the populace had to work at providing a subsistence. A great deal of this work was hard, monotonous and unappealing – and thus required careful apportioning in an egalitarian society.

[26] One would have thought that considerable numbers would also have been employed making such things as pottery, harness, bread and books, or in mining or the merchant marine. Presumably all professionals – doctors, for example – are drawn from the class of scholars (p.53).

permission. When he has learned both, he pursues the one he likes better, unless the city needs one more than the other.[27]

The chief and almost the only business of the syphogrants is to manage matters so that no one sits around in idleness, and to make sure that everyone works hard at his trade. But no one has to exhaust himself with endless toil from early morning to late at night, as if he were a beast of burden. Such wretchedness, really worse than slavery, is the common lot of workmen almost everywhere except in Utopia.[28] Of the day's twenty-four hours, the Utopians devote only six to work. They work three hours before noon, when they go to lunch. After lunch, they rest for a couple of hours, then go to work for another three hours. Then they have supper, and about eight o'clock (counting the first hour after noon as one) they go to bed, and sleep eight hours.

The idle are expelled from society

Workmen not to be overtasked

The other hours of the day, when they are not working, eating, or sleeping, are left to each man's individual discretion, provided he does not waste his free time in roistering or sloth but uses it properly in some occupation that pleases him. Generally these periods are devoted to intellectual activity. For they have an established custom of giving public lectures before daybreak;[29] attendance at these lectures is required only of those who have been specially chosen to devote themselves to learning, but a great many other people of all kinds, both men and women,[30] choose voluntarily to attend. Depending on their interests, some go to one lecture, some to another. But if anyone would rather devote his spare time to his trade, as many do who don't care for the intellectual life, this is not discouraged; in fact, such persons are commended as specially useful to the commonwealth.

The study of letters

---

[27] The fact that all Utopians have at least two occupations (agriculture and one of the crafts), and in some cases three, brings them into implicit conflict with Plato, who strongly insists that in a well-ordered commonwealth each individual would have one and only one profession (*Republic* II.370A-C; *Laws* VIII.846D-E).

[28] In England, for example, an 'Act concerning Artificers & Labourers', 1514–15, made exorbitant demands upon the time of workmen: daybreak to nightfall from mid-September to mid-March; before 5 am to between 7 and 8 pm from mid-March to mid-September (*The Statutes of the Realm*, III (London, 1822), 124–6).

[29] In the universities of More's time, lectures normally began between 5 and 7 am.

[30] Humanists were pioneers in forwarding the education of women. Celibate Erasmus was greatly impressed by the erudite daughters of his married fellow humanists, including Margaret More. See 'The Abbot and the Learned Lady' in Erasmus' *Colloquies*.

Diversion after supper

After supper, they devote an hour to recreation, in their gardens when the weather is fine, or during winter weather in the common halls where they have their meals. There they either play music or

But now gambling is the sport of kings

amuse themselves with conversation. They know nothing about gambling with dice or other such foolish and ruinous games. They do play two games not unlike our own chess. One is a battle of numbers, in which one number captures another. The other is a

Their games are useful too

game in which the vices fight a battle against the virtues. The game is ingeniously set up to show how the vices oppose one another, yet readily combine against the virtues; then, what vices oppose what virtues, how they try to assault them openly or undermine them indirectly; how the virtues can break the strength of the vices or elude their plots; and finally, by what means one side or the other gains the victory.

But in all this, you may get a wrong impression if we don't go back and consider one point more carefully. Because they allot only six hours to work, you might think the necessities of life would be in scant supply. This is far from the case. Their working hours are ample to provide not only enough but more than enough of the necessities and even the conveniences of life. You will easily appre-

Kinds of idlers

ciate this if you consider how large a part of the population in other countries exists without doing any work at all. In the first place, hardly any of the women, who are a full half of the population, work;[31] or, if they do, then as a rule their husbands lie snoring in bed. Then there is a great lazy gang of priests and so-called religious men. Add to them all the rich, especially the landlords, who are commonly called gentlemen and nobility. Include with

Noblemen's bodyguards

them their retainers, that mob of swaggering bullies. Finally, reckon in with these the sturdy and lusty beggars who go about feigning some disease as an excuse for their idleness. You will certainly find

A very shrewd observation

that the things which satisfy our needs are produced by far fewer hands than you had supposed.

And now consider how few of those who do work are doing really essential things. For where money is the measure of everything,

[31] A strange statement, in view of the fact that women had the same, or heavier, domestic duties in the sixteenth century as in the twentieth. In Utopia, they are responsible for some at least of these duties – cooking, childcare – in addition to practising a craft and taking their turn at farm work. Small problems, such as who does the laundry, who cleans the house, who tends the garden, are solved by the simple expedient of not mentioning them.

many vain, superfluous trades are bound to be carried on simply to satisfy luxury and licentiousness. Suppose the multitude of those who now work were limited to a few trades and set to producing just those commodities that nature really requires.[32] They would be bound to produce so much that prices would drop and the workmen would be unable to make a living. But suppose again that all the workers in useless trades were put to useful ones, and that the whole crowd of idlers (each of whom guzzles as much as any two of the workmen who create what they consume) were assigned to productive tasks – well, you can easily see how little time each man would have to spend working, in order to produce all the goods that human needs and conveniences call for – yes, and human pleasure too, as long as it's true and natural pleasure.

The experience of Utopia makes this perfectly apparent. In each city and its surrounding countryside barely five hundred of those men and women whose age and strength make them fit for work are exempted from it.[33] Among these are the syphogrants, who by law are free not to work; yet they don't take advantage of the privilege, preferring to set a good example to their fellow citizens. Some others are permanently exempted from work so that they may devote themselves to study, but only on the recommendation of the priests[34] and through a secret vote of the syphogrants. If any of these scholars disappoints their hopes, he becomes a workman again. On the other hand, it happens from time to time that a craftsman devotes his leisure so earnestly to study, and makes such progress as a result, that he is relieved of manual labour and promoted to the order of learned men. From this class of scholars are chosen ambassadors, priests, tranibors and the prince himself, who used to be called Barzanes, but in their modern tongue is known as Ademos.[35] Since almost all

Not even officials dodge work

Only the learned hold public office

---

[32] The notion that a well-ordered commonwealth would not countenance trades other than those that supply legitimate human needs is traceable to Plato (*Republic* II.372D–373D). Plutarch says that Lycurgus, the lawgiver of Sparta, 'banished the unnecessary and superfluous arts' ('Lycurgus' IX.3).

[33] Two hundred of these are syphogrants; presumably the prince, the twenty tranibors and the thirteen priests (p. 101) are also exempt. The rest must be scholars, and the ambassadors drawn from their ranks.

[34] The priests are in charge of the education of children (p. 102).

[35] 'Barzanes': probably Hebrew *bar*, 'son of', plus *Zanos*, Doric poetic form of the genitive of Zeus. A potent Chaldean magician named Mithrobarzanes figures in Lucian's 'Menippus', which More had translated. 'Ademos': Greek α-privative plus *demos*, 'people': hence 'Peopleless.'

the rest of the populace is neither idle nor engaged in useless trades, it is easy to see why they produce so much in such a short working day.

Apart from all this, in several of the necessary crafts their way of life requires less total labour than does that of people elsewhere. In *Avoiding expense in building* other countries, building and repairing houses demands the constant labour of many men, because what a father has built, his thriftless heir lets fall into ruin; and then his successor has to reconstruct, at great expense, what could easily have been kept up at a very small charge. Again, when a man has built a splendid house at vast cost, someone else may think he has better taste, let the first house fall to ruin, and then build another one somewhere else for just as much money. But among the Utopians, where everything has been well-ordered and the commonwealth properly established, building a new home on a new site is a rare event. They are not only quick to repair deterioration, but foresighted in preventing it. The result is that their buildings last for a very long time with minimum repairs; and the carpenters and masons sometimes have so little to do that they are set to squaring timber and cutting stone for prompt use in case of future need.

Consider, too, how little labour their clothing requires. Their *Avoiding expense in clothing* work clothes are loose garments made of leather or pelts, which last as long as seven years. When they go out in public, they cover these rough work clothes with a cloak. Throughout the entire island, they all wear cloaks of the same colour, which is that of natural wool.[36] As a result, they not only need less wool than people in other countries, but what they do need is less expensive. They use linen cloth most because it requires least labour. They like linen cloth to be white and wool cloth to be clean; but they do not value fineness of texture. Elsewhere a man may not be satisfied with four or five woollen cloaks of different colours and as many silk shirts – or if he's a bit of a fop, even ten of each are not enough. But a Utopian is content with a single cloak, and generally wears it for two years. There is no

---

[36] More's letter to Erasmus of *c.* 4 December 1516 – in which he reports a daydream of being King of Utopia – identifies this garment as a Franciscan cowl (*Selected Letters*, p. 85). The Carthusians, with whom More lived for some years (Introduction, p. xiv), wore garments of undyed wool. The biographical sketch of More that Erasmus included in a letter to Ulrich von Hutten says that 'Simple clothes please ... [More] best, and he never wears silk or scarlet or a gold chain, except when it is not open to him to lay it aside' (*CWE*, VII, 18).

reason why he should want any more garments, for if he had them, he would not be better protected against the cold, nor would he appear in any way better dressed.

When there is an abundance of everything as a result of everyone working at useful trades and nobody consuming to excess, they sometimes assemble great numbers of people to work on the roads, if any need repairs. And when there is no need even for this sort of public work, then the officials very often proclaim a shorter work day, since they never force their citizens to perform useless labour. The chief aim of their constitution is that, as far as public needs permit, all citizens should be free to withdraw as much time as possible from the service of the body and devote themselves to the freedom and culture of the mind. For that, they think, is the real happiness of life.

SOCIAL AND BUSINESS RELATIONS

Now I must explain the social relations of these folk, how the citizens behave towards one another, and how they distribute goods within the society.

Each city, then, consists of households, the households consisting generally of blood-relations. When the women grow up and are married, they move into their husbands' households. On the other hand, male children and their offspring remain in the family, and are subject to the oldest member, unless his mind has started to fail, in which case the next oldest takes his place. To keep the cities from becoming too sparse or too crowded, they have decreed that there shall be six thousand households in each (exclusive of the surrounding countryside), with each household containing between ten and sixteen adults. They do not, of course, try to regulate the number of minor children in a family.[37] The limit on adults is easily observed by transferring individuals from a household with too many into a household with not enough. Likewise if a city has too

The number of citizens

---

[37] If an average household includes thirteen adults, then there are approximately 78,000 adults per city. Those on two-year tours of agricultural duty may or may not be included. Allowing for children and slaves, the population of each Utopian city must be in excess of 100,000, making them larger than all but the greatest European cities of the time.

The closest parallel to the Utopian arrangements is found in Plato's *Laws* (V.740A–741A), where the ideal figure of 5,040 households for the polis is maintained by relocating children, manipulating the birthrate and establishing colonies.

many people, the extra persons serve to make up the shortage of population in other cities. And if the population throughout the entire island exceeds the quota, they enrol citizens out of every city and plant a colony under their own laws on the mainland near them, wherever the natives have plenty of unoccupied and uncultivated land. Those natives who want to live with the Utopians are taken in. When such a merger occurs the two peoples gradually and easily blend together, sharing the same way of life and customs, much to the advantage of both. For by their policies the Utopians make the land yield an abundance for all, though previously it had seemed too barren and paltry even to support the natives. But those who refuse to live under their laws the Utopians drive out of the land they claim for themselves; and on those who resist them, they declare war. The Utopians say it's perfectly justifiable to make war on people who leave their land idle and waste yet forbid the use and possession of it to others who, by the law of nature, ought to be supported from it.

If for any reason the population of one city shrinks so sharply that it cannot be made up without draining others, the numbers are restored by bringing people back from the colonies. This has happened only twice, they say, in their whole history, both times in consequence of a frightful plague. They would rather let their colonies perish entirely than allow any of the cities on their island to get too small.

But to return to their manner of living. The oldest of every household, as I said, is the ruler. Wives act as helpers to their husbands, children to their parents, and generally the younger to their elders. Every city is divided into four equal districts, and in the middle of each district is a market for all kinds of commodities. Whatever each household produces is brought here and stored in warehouses, each kind of goods in its own place. Here the head of every household looks for what he or his family needs and carries off what he wants without any sort of payment or compensation. Why should anything be refused him? There is plenty of everything, and no reason to fear that anyone will claim more than he needs. Why would anyone be suspected of asking for more than is needed, when everyone knows there will never be any shortage? Fear of want, no doubt, makes every living creature greedy and avaricious, and man, besides, develops these qualities out of pride, which glories in putting down

Thus they eliminate crowds of idle servants

The sources of greed

56

others by a superfluous display of possessions. But this sort of vice has no place whatever in the Utopian way of life.

Next to the marketplace of which I just spoke are the food markets, where people bring all sorts of vegetables, fruit and bread. Fish, meat and poultry are also brought there from designated places outside the city, where running water can carry away all the blood and refuse. Bondsmen do the slaughtering and cleaning in these places: citizens are not allowed to do such work.[38] The Utopians feel that slaughtering our fellow creatures gradually destroys the sense of compassion, the finest sentiment of which our human nature is capable. Besides, they don't allow anything dirty or filthy to be brought into the city lest the air become tainted by putrefaction and thus infectious.[39]

Filth and garbage spread disease in cities

By butchering beasts we learn to slaughter men

Every ward has its own spacious halls, equally distant from one another, and each known by a special name. In these halls live the syphogrants. Thirty families are assigned to each hall – fifteen from each side of it – to take their meals in common.[40] The stewards of all the halls meet at a fixed time in the market and get food according to the number of persons for whom each is responsible.

In distributing food, first consideration goes to the sick, who are cared for in public hospitals. Every city has four of these, built at the city limits slightly outside the walls, and spacious enough to appear like little towns. The hospitals are large for two reasons: so that the sick, however numerous they may be, will not be packed closely and uncomfortably together, and also so that those with contagious diseases, such as might pass from one to the other, may be isolated. The hospitals are well ordered and supplied with everything needed to cure the patients, who are nursed with tender and watchful care. Highly skilled physicians are in constant attendance. Consequently, though nobody is sent there against his will, there is hardly

Caring for the sick

---

[38] The bondsmen (Latin *famuli*), who are mentioned only here, should perhaps be distinguished from the slaves (Latin *servi*) who are referred to several times. But on p. 73 Hythloday notes that the Utopians have assigned hunting 'to their butchers, who, as I said before, are all slaves' (*servi*).

[39] In the cramped cities of the time, this rule was necessary (though not, of course, because filth makes the air infectious). Even in modern times, slaughterhouses are still generally located in the outskirts.

[40] According to Plutarch, Lycurgus instituted the common messes of Sparta as part of his plan 'to attack luxury ... and remove the thirst for wealth' ('Lycurgus' x). For similar reasons the institution was incorporated into the ideal commonwealths of Plato and Aristotle (*Republic* III.416E; *Politics* VII.x.10).

anyone in the city who would not rather be treated for an illness at the hospital than at home.

When the hospital steward has received the food prescribed for the sick by their doctors, the best of the remainder is fairly divided among the halls according to the number in each, except that special regard is paid to the prince, the high priest and the tranibors, as well as to ambassadors and foreigners, if there are any. In fact, foreigners are very few; but when they do come, they have certain furnished

Meals in common, mixing all groups

houses assigned to them. At the hours of lunch and supper, a brazen trumpet summons the entire syphogranty to assemble in their hall, except for those who are bedridden in the hospitals or at home. After

Note how freedom is granted everywhere, lest people act under compulsion

the halls have been served with their quotas of food, nothing prevents an individual from carrying home something extra for himself from the marketplace. They realise that no one would do this without good reason. For while it is not forbidden to eat at home, no man does it willingly because it is not thought proper; and besides, a man would be stupid to work at preparing a worse meal at home when he had a sumptuous one near at hand in the hall.

In the syphogrant's hall, slaves do all the particularly dirty and

Women prepare the meals

heavy chores. But planning the meal, as well as preparing and cooking the food, is carried out by the women alone, with each family taking its turn. Depending on the number, they sit down at three or more tables. The men sit with their backs to the wall, the women on the outside, so that if a woman has a sudden qualm or pain, such as occasionally happens during pregnancy, she may get up without disturbing the others, and go off to the nurses.

A separate dining room is assigned to the nurses and infants, with a plentiful supply of cradles, clean water and a warm fire. Thus the nurses may lay the infants down, change them and let them play before the fire. Each child is nursed by its own mother, unless death or illness prevents. When that happens, the wife of the syphogrant quickly finds a suitable nurse. The problem is not difficult: any woman who can volunteers gladly for the job, since everyone

Honour and praise incite people to act properly

applauds her kindness, and the child itself regards its new nurse as its natural mother.

Children under the age of five sit together in the nursery. All

Raising the young

other minors, both boys and girls up to the age of marriage, either wait on table, or, if not old and strong enough for that, stand by in

absolute silence. They eat whatever is handed to them by those sitting at the table, and have no other set time for their meals.

At the middle of the first table in the highest part of the dining hall
sits the syphogrant with his wife. This is the place of greatest
honour, and from this table, which is placed crosswise of the hall,
the whole gathering can be seen. Two of the eldest sit with them – *Priest before*
for the seating is always by groups of four. But if there is a church in *prince. But now*
the district, the priest and his wife sit with the syphogrant so as to *even bishops act as servants to royalty*
preside. On both sides of them sit younger people, next to them *Young mixed with*
older people again, and so through the hall: thus those of about the *old*
same age sit together, yet are mingled with others of a different age.
The reason for this, as they explain it, is that the dignity of the aged,
and the respect due to them, may restrain the younger people from
improper freedom of words or gestures, since nothing said or done
at table can pass unnoticed by the old, who are present on every side.

Dishes of food are not served down the tables in order from top to
bottom, but all the old persons, who are seated in conspicuous *Respect for the*
places, are served first with the best food, and then equal shares are *elderly*
given to the rest. The old people, as they feel inclined, give their
neighbours a share of those delicacies which were not plentiful
enough to be served to everyone. Thus due respect is paid to senior-
ity, yet the principle of equality is preserved.

They begin every lunch and supper with some reading on a moral *Not even monks do*
topic, but keep it brief lest it become a bore. Taking that as an *this now*
occasion, the elders introduce topics of conversation,[41] which they *Table talk*
try not to make gloomy or dull. They never monopolise the conversation with long monologues, but are ready to hear what the young
men say. In fact, they deliberately draw them out, in order to discover the natural temper and quality of each one's mind, as revealed
in the freedom of mealtime talk.

Their lunches are light, their suppers rather more elaborate, *Modern doctors*
because lunch is followed by work, supper by rest and a night's *think ill of this practice*
sleep, which they think particularly helpful to good digestion. No
evening meal passes without music, and the dessert course is never *Music at*
scanted; during the meal, they burn incense and scatter perfume, *mealtimes*
omitting nothing which will make the occasion festive. For they are

[41] Humanists were fond of this ancient social custom – which, as the gloss implies,
lingered longest in the monasteries. Stapleton says it was the practice at More's table
(*The Life and Illustrious Martyrdom of Sir Thomas More*, p. 89).

*Innocent pleasures
are not to be
rejected* much inclined to think that no kind of pleasure is forbidden, provided harm does not come of it.

This is the pattern of life in the city; but in the country, where they
are farther removed from neighbours, they all eat in their own
homes. No family lacks for food since, after all, whatever city-
dwellers eat comes originally from those in the country.

THE TRAVELS OF THE UTOPIANS

Anyone who wants to visit friends in another city, or simply to see the
place itself, can easily obtain permission from his syphogrant and
tranibor, unless for some special reason he is needed at home. They
travel together in groups, taking a letter from the prince granting
leave to travel and fixing a day of return. They are given a wagon and
a public slave to drive the oxen and look after them, but unless
women are in the company they dispense with the wagon as an
unnecessary bother. Wherever they go, though they take nothing
with them, they never lack for anything because they are at home
everywhere. If they stay more than a day in one place, each man
practises his trade there, and is kindly received by the local artisans.

Anyone who takes upon himself to leave his district without permission, and is caught without the prince's letter, is treated with
contempt, brought back as a runaway, and severely punished. If he
is bold enough to try it a second time, he is made a slave. Anyone
who wants to stroll about and explore the extent of his own district is
not prevented, provided he first obtains his father's permission and
his wife's consent. But wherever he goes in the countryside, he gets
no food until he has completed either a morning's or an afternoon's
stint of work.[42] On these terms he may go where he pleases within
his own district, yet be just as useful to the community as if he were at
home.

*O sacred society,
worthy of
imitation,
especially by
Christians!* So you see there is no chance to loaf or kill time, no pretext for
evading work; there are no wine-bars, or ale-houses, or brothels; no
chances for corruption; no hiding places; no spots for secret meetings. Because they live in the full view of all, they are bound to be
either working at their usual trades or enjoying their leisure in a re-

---

[42] The Utopians in this rule agree with St Paul: II Thessalonians 3:10.

spectable way. Such customs must necessarily result in plenty of
life's good things, and since they share everything equally, it follows
that no one can ever be reduced to poverty or forced to beg.

Equality for all results in enough for each

In the annual gathering at Amaurot (to which, as I said before,
three representatives come from each city), they survey the island to
find out where there are shortages and surpluses, and promptly
satisfy one district's shortage with another's surplus. These are
outright gifts; those who give get nothing in return from those who
receive. Though they give freely to one city, they get freely from
another to which they gave nothing; and thus the whole island is like
a single family.[43]

The commonwealth is nothing but a kind of extended family

After they have accumulated enough for themselves – and this
they consider to be a full two-years' store, because next year's crop is
always uncertain – then they export their surpluses to other countries. They sell abroad great quantities of grain, honey, wool, flax,
timber, scarlet and purple dyestuffs, hides, wax, tallow and leather,
as well as livestock. One seventh of their cargo they give freely to the
poor of the importing country, and the rest they sell at moderate
prices. In exchange they receive, not only such goods as they lack at
home (in fact, about the only important thing they lack is iron), but
immense quantities of silver and gold. They have been carrying on
trade for a long time now, and have accumulated a greater supply of
the precious metals than you would believe possible. As a result, they
now care very little whether they sell for cash or on credit, and most
payments to them actually take the form of promissory notes. However, in all such transactions, they never trust individuals but insist
that the foreign city become officially responsible. When the day of
payment comes, the city collects the money from private debtors,
puts it into the treasury, and enjoys the use of it till the Utopians
claim payment. Most of it, in fact, is never claimed. The Utopians
think it is hardly right to take what they don't need away from people
who do need it. But if they want to lend the money to some other
nation, then they call it in – as they do also when they must wage war.
This is the only reason that they keep such an immense treasure at

Utopian business dealings

Never do they fail to be mindful of the community

How money can be useful

---

[43] According to Plutarch, Lycurgus, returning from a journey just after harvest, and seeing 'the heaps of grain standing parallel and equal to one another, ... said to them that
were by: "All Laconia looks like a family estate newly divided among many brothers"'
('Lycurgus' VIII.4).

home, as a protection against extreme peril or sudden emergency. They use it above all to hire, at extravagant rates of pay, foreign mercenaries, whom they would much rather risk in battle than their own citizens. They know very well that for large enough sums of money many of the enemy's soldiers themselves can be bought off or set at odds with one another, either openly or secretly.

Better to avoid war by bribery or guile than to wage it with great bloodshed

For these reasons, therefore, they have accumulated a vast treasure, but they do not keep it like a treasure. I'm really quite ashamed to tell you how they do keep it, because you probably won't believe me; I would not have believed it myself if someone else had simply told me about it, but I was there and saw it with my own eyes. As a general rule, the more different anything is from what people are used to, the harder it is to accept. But considering that all their other customs are so unlike ours, a sensible man will perhaps not be surprised that they treat gold and silver quite differently from the way we do. After all, they never do use money amongst themselves, but keep it only for a contingency that may or may not actually arise. So in the meanwhile they take care that no one shall value gold and silver, of which money is made, beyond what the metals themselves deserve. Anyone can see, for example, that iron is far superior to either; men could not live without iron, by heaven, any more than without fire or water. But gold and silver have, by nature, no function with which we cannot easily dispense. Human folly has made them precious because they are rare. But in fact nature, like a most indulgent mother, has placed her best gifts out in the open, like air, water and the earth itself; vain and unprofitable things she has hidden away in remote places.

O crafty fellow!

As far as utility goes, gold is inferior to iron

If in Utopia gold and silver were kept locked up in some tower, smart fools among the common people might concoct a story that the prince and senate were out to cheat ordinary folk and get some advantage for themselves. Of course, the gold and silver might be put into beautiful plate-ware and such rich handiwork, but then in case of necessity the people would not want to give up articles on which they had begun to fix their hearts – only to melt them down for soldiers' pay. To avoid these problems they thought of a plan which conforms with their institutions as clearly as it contrasts with our own. Unless one has actually seen it working, their plan may seem incredible, because we prize gold so highly and are so careful about guarding it. With them it's just the other way. While they eat from earthenware dishes and drink from glass cups, finely made but inexpensive, their chamber pots and all their humblest vessels, for use in common halls and even in private homes, are made of gold and silver.[44] The chains and heavy fetters of slaves are also made of these metals. Finally, criminals who are to bear the mark of some disgraceful act are forced to wear golden rings in their ears and on their fingers, golden chains around their necks, even gold crowns on their heads. Thus they hold up gold and silver to scorn in every conceivable way. As a result, if they had to part with their entire supply of these metals, which other people give up with as much agony as if they were being disembowelled, the Utopians would feel it no more than the loss of a penny.

O magnificent scorn for gold!

Gold the mark of infamy

They pick up pearls by the seashore, diamonds and garnets from certain cliffs, but never go out of set purpose to look for them.[45] If they happen to find some, they polish them and give them to the children, who feel proud and pleased with such gaudy decorations when they are small. But after, when they grow a bit older and notice that only babies like such toys, they lay them aside. Their parents don't have to say anything, they simply put these trifles away out of a shamefaced sense that they're no longer suitable, just as our children, when they grow up, put away their marbles, rattles and dolls.

Gems the playthings of children

Different customs, different feelings: I never saw the adage better illustrated than in the case of the Anemolian[46] ambassadors, who came to Amaurot while I was there. Because they came to discuss important business, the senate had assembled ahead of time, three citizens from each city. The ambassadors from nearby nations, who had visited Utopia before and knew the local customs, realised that fine clothing was not much respected in that land, silk was despised, and gold a badge of contempt; therefore they always came in the very

A neat tale

---

[44] More may have got this idea from accounts of primitive societies. Tacitus reports of the ancient Germans that 'One may see among them silver vessels ... treated as of no more value than earthenware' (*Germany* 5). Vespucci notes the Indians' indifference to gold and gems (*Four Voyages*, p. 98), as does the explorer Pietro Martire d'Anghiera (1457–1526), who tells of a tribe that 'used kitchen and other common utensils made of gold' (*On the New World [De Orbe Novo]*, trans. Francis A. MacNutt, 2 vols. (New York and London, 1912), I, 221).

[45] Similarly, Tacitus reports of the ancient Britons that though their sea produces pearls, 'they are gathered only when thrown up on shore' (*Agricola* 12).

[46] From *anemolios*, 'windy'.

plainest of their clothes. But the Anemolians, who lived farther off and had had fewer dealings with the Utopians, had heard only that they all dressed alike and very simply; so they took for granted that their hosts had nothing to wear that they didn't put on. Being themselves rather more proud than wise, they decided to dress as splendidly as the very gods, and dazzle the eyes of the poor Utopians with their gaudy garb.

Consequently the three ambassadors made a grand entry with a suite of a hundred attendants, all in clothing of many colours, and most in silk. Being noblemen at home, the ambassadors were arrayed in cloth of gold, with heavy gold chains round their necks, gold jewels at their ears and on their fingers, and sparkling strings of pearls and gems on their caps. In fact, they were decked out in all the articles which in Utopia are used to punish slaves, shame wrongdoers, or pacify infants. It was a sight to see how they strutted when they compared their finery with the dress of the Utopians who had poured out into the street to see them pass. But it was just as funny to see how wide they fell of the mark, and how far they were from getting the consideration they expected. Except for a very few Utopians who for some special reason had visited foreign countries, all the onlookers considered this splendid pomp a mark of disgrace. They therefore bowed to the humblest servants as lords, and took the ambassadors, because of their golden chains, to be slaves, passing them by without any reverence at all. You might have seen children, who had themselves thrown away their pearls and gems, nudge their mothers when they saw the ambassadors' jewelled caps, and say, 'Look at that big lout, mother, who's still wearing pearls and jewels *The rascal!* as if he were a little kid!' But the mother, in all seriousness, would answer, 'Quiet, son, I think he is one of the ambassadors' fools.'

Others found fault with the golden chains as useless because they were so flimsy any slave could break them, and so loose that he could easily shake them off and run away whenever he wanted.

But after the ambassadors had spent a couple of days among the Utopians, they learned of the immense amounts of gold which were as thoroughly despised there as they were prized at home. They saw too that more gold and silver went into making chains and fetters for a single runaway slave than into costuming all three of them. Somewhat crestfallen, then, they put away all the finery in which they had strutted so arrogantly; but they saw the wisdom of doing so after they had talked with the Utopians enough to learn their customs and opinions.[47]

The Utopians marvel that any mortal can take pleasure in the weak sparkle of a little gem or bright pebble when he has a star, or the sun itself, to look at. They are amazed at the madness of any man who considers himself a nobler fellow because he wears clothing of specially fine wool. No matter how delicate the thread, they say, a sheep wore it once, and still was nothing but a sheep.[48] They are surprised that gold, a useless commodity in itself, is everywhere valued so highly that man himself, who for his own purposes conferred this value on it, is far less valuable. They do not understand why a dunderhead with no more brains than a post, and who is about as lewd as he is foolish, should command a great many wise and good people, simply because he happens to have a big pile of gold. Yet if this booby should lose his money to the lowest rascal in his household (as can happen by chance or through some legal trick – for the law can produce reversals as violent as luck itself), he would promptly become one of the fellow's scullions, as if he were personally attached to the coin, and a mere appendage to it. Even more than this, the Utopians are appalled at those people who practically worship a rich man, though they neither owe him anything nor are under his thumb in any way. What impresses them is simply the fact that the man is rich. Yet all the while they know he is so mean and grasping that as long as he lives not a single tiny penny out of that great mound of money will ever come their way.

These and the like attitudes the Utopians have picked up partly from their upbringing, since the institutions of their community are completely opposed to such folly, partly from instruction and the reading of good books. For though not many people in each city are

'Weak' because the gems are fake, or their glitter is feeble and scanty

How true and how apt!

How much wiser are the Utopians than the ruck of Christians

---

[47] The story of the Anemolian ambassadors owes something to Lucian's 'The Wisdom of Nigrinus', in which a visiting millionaire makes a fool of himself by stalking around Athens in a purple robe: 'with his crowd of attendants and his gay clothes and jewelry, ... [he] expected to be looked up to as a happy man. But they thought the creature unfortunate, and undertook to educate him ... His gay clothes and his purple gown they stripped from him very neatly by making fun of his flowery colours, saying "Spring already?" "How did that peacock get here?" "Perhaps it's his mother's" and the like' (sect. 13).

[48] The source is Lucian's 'Demonax' (sect. 41). More repeated the idea years later in *A Treatise upon the Passion of Christ* (1534) (*CW*, XIII, 8).

excused from labour and assigned to scholarship full time (these are persons who from childhood have given evidence of excellent character, unusual intelligence and devotion to learning), every child gets an introduction to good literature, and throughout their lives many people, men and women alike, spend their free time in reading.

Training and studies of the Utopians

They study all the branches of learning in their native tongue, which is not deficient in terminology or unpleasant in sound, and adapts itself as well as any to the expression of thought. That entire area of the world uses just about the same language, though elsewhere it is more corrupt, depending on the district.

Before we came there the Utopians had never so much as heard about a single one of those philosophers[49] whose names are so cele-

Music, dialectic and mathematics

brated in our part of the world. Yet in music, dialectic, arithmetic and geometry[50] they have found out just about the same things as our great men of the past. But while they equal the ancients in almost all other subjects, they are far from matching the inventions of our

The passage seems a bit satiric

modern logicians.[51] In fact they have not discovered even one of those elaborate rules about restrictions, amplifications and suppositions which our own schoolboys study in the *Small Logicals*. They are so far from being able to speculate on 'second intentions'[52] that not one of them was able to conceive of 'man-in-general', though I pointed straight at him with my finger, and he is, as you well know,

---

[49] As the following sentence indicates, 'philosophers' is used here in the old, broad sense that includes those learned in the physical and mathematical sciences as well as students of metaphysics and moral philosophy.

[50] Music, arithmetic and geometry, together with astronomy (below), constitute the advanced division – the *quadrivium* – of the traditional Seven Liberal Arts. Dialectic joins with grammar and rhetoric to constitute the elementary division – the *trivium*. Grammar and rhetoric would be encompassed in the Utopians' study of 'good literature'.

[51] I.e., the scholastic philosophers. The *Small Logicals* (below) is probably the *Parva logicalia* of Peter of Spain (d. 1277), though more than one textbook bore this name. In his long open letter to the theologian and philologist Maarten van Dorp, More complains that 'a type of nonsense, worse than that of the sophists, has gradually displaced [genuine] dialectics'. The *Small Logicals*, 'so called, I suppose, because it has very little logic in it, is worth while looking at, with its suppositions, as they are called, its ampliations, restrictions, and appellations, and passages in which occur little rules, not only silly, but even false' (*Selected Letters*, pp. 20–1).

[52] 'First intentions' are the direct apprehensions of things; 'second intentions' are purely abstract conceptions, derived from considering the relations of first intentions.

bigger than any giant, maybe even a colossus.[53] On the other hand, they have learned to plot expertly the courses of the stars and the movements of the heavenly bodies. To this end they have devised a number of different instruments by which they compute with the greatest exactness the course of the sun, the moon and the other stars that are visible in their area of the sky. As for the friendly and hostile influences of the planets and that whole deceitful business of divination by the stars, they have never so much as dreamed of it. From long experience in observation, they are able to forecast rains, winds and other changes in the weather. But as to the causes of the weather, of the tides in the sea and its saltiness, and the origins and nature of the heavens and the earth, they have various opinions. Generally they treat of these matters as our ancient philosophers did, but they also disagree with one another, as the ancients did, nor do they have any generally accepted theory of their own.

The study of the stars

Yet these astrologers are revered by Christians to this very day

Physics the most uncertain study of all

In matters of moral philosophy, they carry on the same arguments as we do. They inquire into the nature of the good, distinguishing goods of the mind from goods of the body and external gifts.[54] They ask whether the name of 'good' can be applied to all three, or whether it refers only to goods of the mind.[55] They discuss virtue and pleasure, but their chief concern is human happiness, and whether it consists of one thing or many.[56] They seem rather too much inclined to the view that all or the most important part of

Ethics

Higher and lower goods

Supreme goods

---

[53] The Utopians' blindness to 'man-in-general' (i.e., man as a 'universal') makes them just opposite to the scholastic philosophers mocked by Erasmus' Folly, who 'on occasion do not see the ditch or the stone lying across their path, because many of them are blear-eyed or absent-minded; yet they proclaim that they perceive ideas, universals, forms without matter, primary substances, quiddities, and ecceities' (*The Praise of Folly*, p. 77).

[54] This threefold classification of goods appears in Plato (*Laws* III.697B, V.743E), but is especially associated with Aristotle (*Nicomachean Ethics* I.viii.2, *Politics* VII.i.3–4) and Aristotelian tradition. Of course the Utopians have never heard of Plato, Aristotle, or any other European philosopher, and one point of the account of Utopian philosophy is that natural reason will lead earnest, ingenious thinkers to the same set of problems and positions at any time and place. The other, main point is to argue that the moral norms derivable from reason are consistent with those of Christianity.

[55] The first position is especially that of the Aristotelians, the second that of the Stoics.

[56] The topics of virtue and pleasure are linked especially in discussions – like Cicero's *On the Supreme Good and Evil* – of the relative merits of Stoic and Epicurean ethics. The idea that happiness is the end of life is axiomatic in all the major philosophical schools.

The Utopians consider honest pleasure the measure of happiness

human happiness consists of pleasure.[57] And what is more surprising, they seek support for this comfortable opinion from their religion, which is serious and strict, indeed, almost stern and forbidding.

First principles of philosophy to be sought in religion

For they never discuss happiness without joining to their philosophic rationalism certain principles of religion. Without these religious principles, they think that reason is bound to prove weak and defective in its efforts to investigate true happiness.

Utopian theology

The immortality of the soul, on which nowadays no small number even of Christians have their doubts

The religious principles they invoke are of this nature: that the soul of man is immortal, and by God's goodness born for happiness; and that after this life, rewards are appointed for our virtues and good deeds, punishments for our sins. Though these are indeed religious beliefs, they think that reason leads men to believe and accept them.[58] And they add unhesitatingly that if these beliefs were rejected, no one would be so stupid as not to feel that he should seek pleasure, regardless of right and wrong. His only care would be to keep a lesser pleasure from standing in the way of a greater one, and

---

[57] I.e., the Utopians are inclined to the Epicurean position. The remark launches a long passage that constitutes, as Edward L. Surtz points out (*The Praise of Pleasure*, pp. 9–11), a praise of pleasure reminiscent of Erasmus' praise of folly. The praise of pleasure, and of Epicurus, had an important precedent in Lorenzo Valla's *On the True and the False Good* (1444–9), which in its original version (1431) was called *On Pleasure*. Valla's work furthered the gradual humanist rehabilitation of Epicurus that began with Petrarch and Boccaccio and in which (after Valla) Ficino, Pico and Erasmus played a part: these writers argued that, contrary to popular opinion, Epicurus did not mean by 'pleasure' mere sensuality. See, in addition to Surtz, D. C. Allen, 'The Rehabilitation of Epicurus and His Theory of Pleasure in the Early Renaissance' (*Studies in Philology*, 41 (1944), 1–15); Edgar Wind, *Pagan Mysteries in the Renaissance*, rev. edn (New York, 1968), pp. 48–71; and George M. Logan, *The Meaning of More's 'Utopia'*, pp. 144–7, 154–63. Vespucci's observation about the Indians may also be relevant: 'Since their life is so entirely given over to pleasure, I should style it Epicurean' (*Four Voyages*, p. 97; see also *New World*, p. 6).

[58] Thomistic theology supports this view. As Surtz observes, Aquinas maintains that 'man, without supernatural grace, can come to the knowledge ... of moral and religious truths, such as the existence and perfections of God, the immortality and spirituality of the soul, the duties of man toward his Creator, and the punishments and rewards of the future life' ('Interpretations of *Utopia*', *Catholic Historical Review*, 38 (1952), 163). In *A Dialogue Concerning Heresies* (1529), More says that 'all the whole number of the old philosophers ... found out by nature and reason that there was a god either maker or governor or both of all this whole engine of the world' (*CW*, VI, 73).

Since Epicurus maintained the indifference of the gods and the mortality of the soul, these principles sharply distinguish Utopian philosophy from classical Epicureanism, and lead the Utopians to a view of the good life similar to the Christian view.

to avoid pleasures that are inevitably followed by pain.[59] Without religious principles, a man would have to be actually crazy to pursue harsh and painful virtue, give up the pleasures of life, and suffer pain from which he can expect no advantage. For if there is no reward after death, a man has no compensation for having passed his entire existence without pleasure, that is, miserably.[60]

To be sure, the Utopians think happiness is found, not in every kind of pleasure, but only in good and honest pleasure. Virtue itself, they say, draws our nature to pleasure of this sort, as to the supreme good. There is an opposed school which declares that virtue is itself happiness.[61]

They define virtue as living according to nature; and God, they say, created us to that end. When a man obeys the dictates of reason in choosing one thing and avoiding another, he is following nature.[62] Now the first rule of reason is to love and venerate the Divine Majesty to whom men owe their existence and every happiness of which they are capable. The second rule of nature is to lead a life as free of anxiety and as full of joy as possible, and to help all one's fellow men towards that end. The most hard-faced eulogist of virtue and the grimmest enemy of pleasure, while they invite us to toil and sleepless nights and mortification, still admonish us to

Not every pleasure is desirable, neither is pain to be sought, except for the sake of virtue

This is like Stoic doctrine

---

[59] This is the first of three citations of Epicurus' rules for choosing between competing pleasures (see Introduction, p. xxvii). The rules find perhaps their most influential statement in Cicero's dialogue *On the Supreme Good and Evil*, where the Epicurean Torquatus explains that 'The wise man always holds ... to this principle of selection: he rejects pleasures to secure other greater pleasures, or else he endures pains to avoid worse pains' (I.x.33; cf. I.x.36). Another formulation occurs in a letter of Epicurus quoted by Diogenes Laertius: 'since pleasure is our first and native good, for that reason we do not choose every pleasure whatsoever, but ofttimes pass over many pleasures when a greater annoyance ensues from them' (*Lives of Eminent Philosophers* X.129). The Utopians accept these rules of selection, but recognise that their application leads to quite different conclusions about the good life depending on whether religious principles are factored into the individual's calculations.

[60] The Utopians, that is, reject the claim that purely rational and mundane considerations provide sufficient sanction for moral behaviour.

[61] This second position is that of the Stoics, who declared that virtue is happiness, whether it leads to pleasure or not – indeed, that a man who is enduring great misery may derive happiness from his knowledge of his own virtuous behaviour. As the following marginal gloss points out, the Utopians' definition of virtue is also Stoic. See, for example, Cicero's *On the Supreme Good and Evil* III.ix.31.

[62] Throughout the ensuing discussion, 'reason' has the sense of 'right reason' – the faculty that, according to a conception passed on by the Stoics to the Middle Ages and the Renaissance, enables men to distinguish right and wrong with instinctive clarity; that is, to apprehend the natural law.

relieve the poverty and misfortune of others as best we can. It is especially praiseworthy, they tell us, when we provide for the comfort and welfare of our fellow creatures. Nothing is more humane (and humanity is the virtue most proper to human beings) than to relieve the misery of others, assuage their griefs, and by removing all sadness from their lives, to restore them to enjoyment, that is, pleasure. Well, if this is the case, why doesn't nature equally invite

But now some people cultivate pain as if it were the essence of religion, rather than incidental to performance of a pious duty or the result of natural necessity – and thus to be borne, not pursued

us to do the same thing for ourselves? Either a joyful life (that is, one of pleasure) is a good thing, or it isn't. If it isn't, then you should not help anyone to it – indeed, you ought to take it away from everyone you can, as harmful and deadly to them. But if such a life is good, and if we are supposed, indeed obliged, to help others to it, why not first of all ourselves, to whom we owe no less charity than to anyone else? When nature prompts us to be kind to our neighbours, she does not mean that we should be cruel and merciless to ourselves. Thus, they say, nature herself prescribes for us a joyous life, in other words, pleasure, as the goal of our actions; and living according to her rules is to be defined as virtue. And as nature bids men to make one another's lives cheerful, as far as they can, so she repeatedly warns you not to seek your own advantage in ways that cause misfortune to others. And this is right; for no man is placed so far above the rest that he is nature's sole concern; she cherishes alike all those living beings to whom she has granted the same form.

Contracts and laws

Consequently, the Utopians say that men should abide not only by private agreements but by those public laws which control the distribution of vital goods, such as are the very substance of pleasure. Any such laws, when properly promulgated by a good king, or ratified by a people free of force and fraud, should be observed; and so long as they are observed, to pursue your own interests is prudence; to pursue the public interest as well is piety; but to pursue your own pleasure by depriving others of theirs is injustice. On the other hand, deliberately to decrease your own pleasure to augment

Mutual assistance

that of others is a work of humanity and benevolence, which never fails to reward the doer over and above his sacrifice. You may be repaid for your kindness, and in any case you are conscious of having done a good deed. Your mind draws more joy from recalling the gratitude and good will of those whom you have benefited than your body would have drawn pleasure from the things you forfeited. Finally, they believe (as religion easily persuades a well-disposed mind to believe) that God will recompense us for surrendering a brief and transitory pleasure here with immense and never-ending joy in heaven. And so they conclude, after carefully considering and weighing the matter, that all our actions and the virtues exercised within them look towards pleasure and happiness as their final end.[63]

By pleasure they understand every state or movement of body or mind in which man finds delight according to nature.[64] 'According to nature' they say, and with good reason. By simply following his senses and his right reason a man may discover what is pleasant by nature: it is a delight that does not injure others, does not preclude a greater pleasure, and is not followed by pain. But a pleasure which is against nature, and which men call 'delightful' only by the emptiest of fictions (as if one could change the real nature of things just by changing their names), does not really make for happiness; in fact, they say it precludes happiness. And the reason is that men whose minds are filled with false ideas of pleasure have no room left for true and genuine delight. For there are a great many things which have no genuine sweetness in them, but are actually bitter – yet which, through the perverse enticements of evil lusts, are considered very great pleasures, and even the supreme goals of life. *What is pleasure?*

False pleasures

Among the pursuers of this false pleasure, the Utopians include those whom I mentioned before, the people who think themselves finer folk because they wear finer clothes. These people are twice mistaken: first in supposing their clothes better than anyone else's, and then in thinking themselves better because of their clothes. As far as a coat's usefulness goes, why is fine woollen thread better than thick? Yet they act as if they were set apart by nature herself, rather than their own fantasies; they strut about and put on airs. Because they have a fancy suit, they think themselves entitled to honours they would never have expected if they were plainly dressed, and grow indignant if someone passes them by without showing special respect. *Mistaken pride in fancy dress*

Isn't it the same kind of absurdity to be pleased by empty, cere-

---

[63] This is Epicurus' view, as reported by Diogenes Laertius: 'we choose the virtues too on account of pleasure and not for their own sake' (X.138).

[64] Both Plato (*Philebus* 36C–52B) and Aristotle (*Nicomachean Ethics* I.viii.11, VII.v.1) acknowledge the importance to the good life of physical as well as mental pleasures, and distinguish between true pleasures – which are 'pleasant by nature' – and false ones. The ensuing discussion relies heavily on these passages.

Foolish titles monial honours? What true or natural pleasure can you get from
someone's bent knee or bared head? Will the creaks in your own
knees be eased thereby, or the madness in your head? The phantom
of false pleasure is illustrated by other men who run mad with
delight over their own blue blood, flatter themselves on their nobility, and gloat over all their rich ancestors (the only sort of nobility
Empty nobility worth claiming these days), and all their ancient family estates. Even
if they don't have the shred of an estate themselves, or if they've
squandered every penny of their inheritance, they don't consider
themselves a bit less noble.[65]

*The silliest
pleasures of all:
gemstones* In the same class the Utopians put those people I described
before, who are mad for jewellery and gems, and think themselves
divinely happy if they find a good specimen, especially of the sort
*Popular opinion
gives gems their
value or takes it
away* that happens to be fashionable in their country at the time – for
stones vary in value from one market to another. The collector will
not make an offer for the stone till it's taken out of its setting, and
even then he will not buy unless the dealer guarantees and gives
security that it is a true and genuine stone. What he fears is that his
eyes will be deceived by a counterfeit. But if you consider the matter,
why should a counterfeit give any less pleasure, when your eyes cannot distinguish it from a genuine gem? Both should be of equal
value to you, as they would be, in reality, to a blind man.[66]

Speaking of false pleasure, what about those who pile up money,
not for any real purpose, but just to sit and look at it? Is that a true
pleasure, or aren't they simply cheated by a show of pleasure? Or
what of those with the opposite vice, who hide away money they will
never use and perhaps never even see again? In their anxiety to hold
on to their money, they actually lose it. For what else happens when
you deprive yourself, and perhaps other people too, of a chance to
use your money by burying it in the ground? And yet, when you've
hidden your treasure away, you exult over it as if, your mind now at
*A strange fancy,
and much to the
point* ease, you could jump for joy. Suppose someone stole it, and you
died ten years later, knowing nothing of the theft. During all those

[65] This passage – like the catalogue of false pleasures as a whole – is close in substance
and tone to *The Praise of Folly*. Folly comments on 'those who, while differing in no
respect from the meanest tinker, flatter themselves beyond measure with the empty title
of nobility' (p. 59).
[66] Erasmus' Folly tells how More 'gave his young wife some imitation jewels as a present,
persuading her – for he is a plausible joker – that they were not only genuine and natural but also of unique and inestimable value' (*The Praise of Folly*, p. 64).

ten years, what did it matter to you whether the money was stolen or not? In either case, it was equally useless to you.

To these false and foolish pleasures they add gambling, which they have heard about, though they've never tried it, as well as hunting and hawking. What pleasure can there be, they wonder, in *Dicing* throwing dice on a table? If there were any pleasure in the action, wouldn't doing it over and over again quickly make one tired of it? What pleasure can there be in listening to the barking and yelping of dogs – isn't that rather a disgusting noise? Is there any more real *Hunting* pleasure when a dog chases a rabbit than when a dog chases a dog? If what you like is fast running, there's plenty of that in both cases; they're just about the same. But if what you really want is slaughter, if you want to see a living creature torn apart under your eyes, then the whole thing is wrong. You ought to feel nothing but pity when you see the hare fleeing from the hound, the weak creature tormented by the stronger, the fearful and timid beast brutalised by the savage one, the harmless hare killed by the cruel hound. The Uto- *Yet today this is* pians, who regard this whole activity of hunting as unworthy of free *the chosen art of* men, have accordingly assigned it to their butchers, who, as I said *our court-* before, are all slaves. In their eyes, hunting is the lowest thing even *divinities* butchers can do. In the slaughterhouse, their work is more useful and honest, since there they kill animals only out of necessity; whereas the hunter seeks nothing but his own pleasure from killing and mutilating some poor little creature. Taking such relish in the sight of death, even if only of beasts, reveals, in the opinion of the Utopians, a cruel disposition. Or if he isn't cruel to start with, the hunter eventually becomes so through the constant practice of such brutal pleasures.[67]

Common opinion considers these activities, and countless others like them, to be pleasures; but the Utopians say flatly they have nothing at all to do with real pleasure, since there's nothing naturally pleasant about them. They often please the senses, and in this they are like pleasure, but that does not alter their basic nature. The enjoyment doesn't arise from the experience itself, but from the

[67] So Folly mocks those who 'feel an ineffable pleasure in their souls whenever they hear the raucous blast of the horns and the yelping of the hounds', and who 'with their butchering and eating of beasts ... accomplish nothing at all unless it be to degenerate into beasts themselves' (*The Praise of Folly*, pp. 53, 54). By contrast, hunting is praised as good exercise and good practice for war by Plato (*Laws* VII.823B–824B) and other classical and later writers, including many of More's and Erasmus' fellow humanists.

73

perverse mind of the individual, as a result of which he mistakes the
Morbid tastes of bitter for the sweet, just as pregnant women whose taste has been
pregnant women distorted sometimes think pitch and tallow taste better than honey. A
man's taste may be similarly depraved, by disease or by custom, but
that doesn't change the nature of pleasure or of anything else.

Varieties of true They distinguish several classes of true pleasure, some being
pleasure pleasures of the mind and others pleasures of the body. Those of the
mind are knowledge and the delight that arises from contemplating
the truth, also the gratification of looking back on a well-spent life
and the unquestioning hope of happiness to come.

Bodily pleasures Pleasures of the body they also divide into two classes. The first is
that which fills the senses with immediate delight. Sometimes this
happens when organs that have been weakened by natural heat are
restored with food and drink; sometimes it happens when we eliminate some excess in the body, as when we move our bowels, generate
children, or relieve an itch somewhere by rubbing or scratching it.
Now and then pleasure arises, not from restoring a deficiency or
discharging an excess, but from something that excites our senses
with a hidden but unmistakable force, and attracts them to itself.
Such is the power of music.

The second kind of bodily pleasure they describe as nothing but
the calm and harmonious state of the body, its state of health when
undisturbed by any disorder. Health itself, when not oppressed by
pain, gives pleasure, without any external excitement at all. Even
though it appeals less directly to the senses than the gross gratifica-
tions of eating and drinking, many consider this to be the greatest
pleasure of all. Most of the Utopians regard this as the foundation of
all the other pleasures, since by itself alone it can make life peaceful
To enjoy anything, and desirable, whereas without it there is no possibility of any other
one should be in pleasure. Mere absence of pain, without positive health, they regard
good health as insensibility, not pleasure.

Some[68] have maintained that a stable and tranquil state of health
is not really a pleasure, on the ground that the presence of health
cannot be felt except in contrast to its opposite. The Utopians (who
have arguments of this sort, just as we do) long ago rejected this
opinion. They nearly all agree that health is crucial to pleasure.
Since pain is inherent in disease, they argue, and pain is the bitter

[68] E.g., Plato, *Republic* IX.583C–E.

enemy of pleasure just as disease is the enemy of health, then pleasure must be inherent in quiet good health. Whether pain is the disease itself or just an accompanying effect makes, they say, no real difference. Similarly, whether health is itself a pleasure or simply the cause of pleasure (as fire is the cause of heat), the fact remains that those who have permanent health must also have pleasure.

When we eat, they say, what happens is that health, which was starting to fade, takes food as its ally in the fight against hunger. While our health gains strength, the simple process of returning vigour gives us pleasure and refreshment. If our health feels delight in the struggle, will it not rejoice when the victory has been won? When at last it is restored to its original strength, which was its aim all through the conflict, will it at once become insensible and fail to recognise and embrace its own good? The idea that health cannot be felt they consider completely wrong. What man, when he's awake, can fail to feel that he's in good health – except one who isn't? Is any man so torpid and dull that he won't admit health is delightfully agreeable to him? And what is delight except pleasure under another name?

Among the various pleasures, then, they seek mostly those of the mind, and prize them most highly. The foremost mental pleasures, they believe, arise from practice of the virtues and consciousness of a good life.[69] Among pleasures of the body, they give first place to health. As for eating, drinking and other delights of that sort, they consider them desirable, but only for the sake of health. They are not pleasant in themselves, but only as ways to withstand the insidious attacks of sickness. A wise man would rather escape sickness altogether than have a good cure for it; he would rather prevent pain than find a palliative. And so it would be better not to need this kind of pleasure at all than to be assuaged by it.

Anyone who thinks happiness consists of this sort of pleasure must confess that his ideal life would be one spent in an endless round of hunger, thirst and itching, followed by eating, drinking,

---

[69] The formulation is from Cicero, who in *On Old Age* maintains that 'the most suitable defences of old age are the principles and practice of the virtues, which, if cultivated in every period of life, bring forth wonderful fruits at the close of a long and busy career, not only because they never fail you even at the very end of life ... but also because it is most delightful to have the consciousness of a life well spent and the memory of many deeds worthily performed' (III.9).

scratching and rubbing. Who can fail to see that such an existence is not only disgusting but miserable? These pleasures are certainly the lowest of all, as they are the most adulterate – for they never occur except in connection with the pains that are their contraries.[70] Hunger, for example, is linked to the pleasure of eating, and by no equal law, since the pain is sharper and lasts longer; it precedes the pleasure, and ends only when the pleasure ends with it. So the Utopians think pleasures of this sort should not be highly rated, except as they are necessary to life. Yet they enjoy these pleasures too, and acknowledge gratefully the kindness of Mother Nature, who coaxes her children with allurements and cajolery to do what in any case they must do from harsh necessity. How wretched life would be if the daily diseases of hunger and thirst had to be overcome by bitter potions and drugs, like some other diseases that afflict us less often!

Beauty, strength and agility, as special and pleasant gifts of nature, they joyfully accept. The pleasures of sound, sight and smell they also accept as the special seasonings of life, recognising that nature intended them to be the particular province of man. No other kind of animal contemplates with delight the shape and loveliness of the universe, or enjoys odours (except in the way of searching for food), or distinguishes harmonious from dissonant sounds. But in all their pleasures, the Utopians observe this rule, that the lesser shall not interfere with the greater, and that no pleasure shall carry pain with it as a consequence. If a pleasure is false, they think it will inevitably lead to pain.

Moreover, they think it is crazy for a man to despise beauty of form, to impair his own strength, to grind his vitality down to torpor, to exhaust his body with fasts, to ruin his health and to scorn all other natural delights, unless by so doing he can better serve the welfare of others or the public advantage. Then indeed he may expect a greater reward from God. But otherwise such a man does no one any good. He gains, perhaps, the empty and shadowy reputation of virtue; and no doubt he hardens himself against fantastic adversities which may never occur. But such a person the Utopians

---

[70] The idea that the restorative pleasures are contaminated by being mixed with the opposite pains comes directly from the *Philebus* (46C–D), as does the notion of a life given over to itching and scratching (46D, 47B; cf. *Gorgias* 494B–D).

consider absolutely crazy – cruel to himself, as well as most ungrateful to nature – as if, to avoid being in her debt, he were to reject all her gifts.

This is the way they think about virtue and pleasure. Human reason, they think, can attain to no surer conclusions than these, unless a revelation from heaven should inspire men with holier notions. In all this, I have no time now to consider whether they are right or wrong, and don't feel obliged to do so. I have undertaken only to describe their principles, not to defend them. But of this I am sure, that whatever you think of their ideas, there is not a more excellent people or a more flourishing commonwealth anywhere in the whole world.

Note this and note it well

The happiness of the Utopians, and a description of them

In body they are nimble and lively, and stronger than you would expect from their stature, though they're by no means tiny. Their soil is not very fertile, nor their climate of the best, but they protect themselves against the weather by temperate living, and improve their soil by industry, so that nowhere do grain and cattle flourish more plentifully, nowhere are men more vigorous or liable to fewer diseases. They do all the things that farmers usually do to improve poor soil by hard work and technical knowledge, but in addition they may even transplant a forest from one district to another. They do this, not so much for the sake of better growth, but to make transport easier, by having wood closer to the sea, the rivers, or the cities themselves. For grain is easier than wood to carry by land over a long distance.

The people in general are easy-going, cheerful, clever, and like their leisure. When they must, they can stand heavy labour, but otherwise they are not very fond of it. In intellectual pursuits they are tireless. When they heard from us about the literature and learning of the Greeks (for we thought that, except for the historians and poets, there was nothing in Latin that they would enjoy), it was wonderful to behold how eagerly they sought to be instructed in Greek. We therefore began to study a little of it with them, at first more to avoid seeming lazy than out of any expectation they would profit by it. But after a short trial, their diligence convinced us that our efforts would not be wasted. They picked up the forms of letters so easily, pronounced the language so aptly, memorised it so quickly, and began to recite so accurately, that it seemed like a miracle. Most of our pupils were established scholars, of course, picked for their

The usefulness of the Greek tongue

Their wonderful aptitude for learning

But now clods and dullards are taught letters, while the best minds are corrupted by pleasures

unusual ability and mature minds; and they studied with us, not just of their own free will, but at the command of the senate. Thus in less than three years they had perfect control of the language, and could read the best Greek authors fluently, unless the text was corrupt. I have a feeling they picked up Greek more easily because it was somewhat related to their own tongue. Though their language resembles Persian in most respects, I suspect them of deriving from Greece because, in the names of cities and in official titles, they retain quite a few vestiges of the Greek tongue.

Before leaving on the fourth voyage I placed on board, instead of merchandise, a good-sized packet of books; for I had resolved not to return at all rather than come home soon. Thus they received from me most of Plato's works and many of Aristotle's, as well as Theophrastus' book *On Plants*,[71] though the latter, I'm sorry to say, was somewhat mutilated. During the voyage I carelessly left it lying around, a monkey got hold of it and from sheer mischief ripped a few pages here and there. Of the grammarians they have only Lascaris, for I did not take Theodorus with me, nor any dictionary except that of Hesychius; and they have Dioscorides.[72] They are very fond of Plutarch's writings, and delighted with the witty persiflage of Lucian.[73] Among the poets they have Aristophanes, Homer and Euripides, together with Sophocles in the small Aldine edition.[74] Of the historians they possess Thucydides and Herodotus, as well as Herodian.[75]

As for medical books, a comrade of mine named Tricius Apinatus[76] brought with him some small treatises by Hippocrates, and

---

[71] Theophrastus was a pupil of Aristotle. His views were still current in the Renaissance.

[72] Constantinus Lascaris and Theodorus Gaza wrote Renaissance grammars of Greek. The Greek dictionary of Hesychius (fifth century AD?) was first printed in 1514. Dioscorides (first century AD) wrote a treatise on drugs and herbs (not properly a dictionary), which was printed in 1499.

[73] 'Plutarch's writings' presumably includes the *Moral Essays* as well as the *Parallel Lives* of eminent Greeks and Romans. For Lucian, see Introduction, p. xx–xxi.

[74] The first modern edition of Sophocles was that of Aldus Manutius in 1502. The house of Aldus, where Erasmus lived and worked for a while, was distinguished both for its list of Greek and Latin works and for its contributions to the art of book design.

[75] Thucydides and Herodotus are the great historians of classical Greece. Herodian (*c.* 175–250 AD) wrote a history of the Roman emperors of the second and third centuries.

[76] A learned joke based on a passage in the *Epigrams* of Martial. Martial says of one set of his poems that *Sunt apinae tricaeque*: 'They're trifles and toys' (XIV.i).

that summary of Galen known as *Microtechne*.[77] They were delighted to have these books because they consider medicine one of the finest and most useful parts of knowledge, even though there's hardly a country in the world that needs doctors less. They think when they thus explore the secrets of nature they are gratifying not only themselves but the author and maker of nature. They suppose that like other artists he created this visible mechanism of the world to be admired – and by whom, if not by man, who is alone in being able to appreciate such an intricate object? Therefore he is bound to prefer a careful observer and sensitive admirer of his work before one who, like a brute beast, looks on the grand spectacle with a stupid and blockish mind.

Medicine most useful of all studies

Contemplation of nature

Once stimulated by learning, the minds of the Utopians are wonderfully quick to seek out those various arts which make life more agreeable and convenient. Two inventions, to be sure, they owe to us: the art of printing and the manufacture of paper. At least they owe these arts partly to us, and in some measure to their own cleverness. While we were showing them the Aldine editions of various books, we talked about paper-making and type-cutting, though without going into details, for none of us had had any practical experience. But with great sharpness of mind they immediately grasped the basic principles. While previously they had written only on vellum, bark and papyrus, they now undertook to make paper and print with type. Their first attempts were not altogether successful, but with practice they soon mastered both arts. If they had the texts of the Greek authors, they would soon have no lack of volumes; but as they have no more than those I mentioned, they have contented themselves with reprinting each in thousands of copies.

Any sightseer coming to their land who has some special intellectual gift, or who has travelled widely and seen many countries, is sure of a warm welcome, for they love to hear what is happening throughout the world. This is why we were received so kindly. Few merchants, however, go there to trade. What could they import, except iron – or else gold and silver, which everyone would rather take home than send abroad? As for the export trade, the Utopians prefer to do their own transportation, instead of letting strangers come to fetch the goods. By carrying their own cargoes, they are able

---

[77] Hippocrates (fifth century BC) and Galen (second century AD) were the most influential Greek medical writers.

to learn more about their neighbours and keep their own navigational skills from getting rusty.

SLAVES

The wonderful fairness of these people The Utopians keep as slaves only prisoners taken in wars fought by the Utopians themselves.[78] The children of slaves are not born into slavery,[79] nor are any slaves imported from foreign countries. Most are either their own citizens, enslaved for some heinous offence, or else foreigners who had been condemned to death in their own land; the latter sort predominate. Sometimes the Utopians buy them at a very modest rate, more often they ask for them, get them for nothing, and bring them home in considerable numbers. Both kinds of slaves are not only kept constantly at work, but are always fettered. The Utopians, however, deal more harshly with their own people than with the others, feeling that their crimes are worse and deserve stricter punishment because, as it is argued, they had an excellent education and the best of moral training, yet still couldn't be restrained from wrongdoing.[80] A third class of slaves consists of hard-working penniless drudges from other nations who voluntarily choose to take service in Utopia. Such people are treated fairly, almost as well as citizens, except that they are assigned a little extra work, on the score that they're used to it. If one of them wants to leave, which seldom happens, no obstacles are put in his way, nor is he sent off empty-handed.

The sick As I said before, the sick are carefully tended, and nothing is neglected in the way of medicine or diet which might cure them. Everything possible is done to mitigate the pain of those suffering from incurable diseases; and visitors do their best to console them by sitting and talking with them. But if the disease is not only incurable, but excruciatingly and unremittingly painful, then the priests and

[78] In classical times prisoners of war – civilians as well as soldiers – constituted a major source of slaves. By More's day there was general agreement that it was wrong for Christians to enslave Christian captives; but non-Christians – especially Africans and American Indians – were often regarded as a different matter. A later passage (p. 95) suggests that the Utopians enslave only the defenders of cities they have had to besiege.
[79] The non-hereditary character of Utopian slavery distinguishes it sharply from that of the classical world and from medieval serfdom.
[80] For the same reason, Plato would punish lawbreakers among the citizens of his ideal commonwealth more severely than non-citizens who commit the same crime (*Laws* IX.854E).

public officials come and urge the invalid not to endure further *Deliberate death* agony. They remind him that he is now unequal to any of life's duties, a burden to himself and others; he has really outlived his own death. They tell him he should not let the disease prey on him any longer, but now that life is simply torture and the world a mere prison cell, he should not hesitate to free himself, or let others free him, from the rack of living. This would be a wise act, they say, since for him death puts an end, not to pleasure, but to agony. In addition, he would be obeying the advice of priests, who are interpreters of God's will; thus it will be a pious and holy act.[81]

Those who have been persuaded by these arguments either starve themselves to death or take a drug which frees them from life without any sensation of dying. But they never force this step on a man against his will; nor, if he decides against it, do they lessen their care of him. The man who yields to their arguments, they think, dies an honourable death; but the suicide, who takes his own life without approval of priests and senate, him they consider unworthy of either earth or fire, and they throw his body, unburied and disgraced, into the nearest bog.

Women do not marry till they are eighteen, nor men till they are *Marriages* twenty-two. Clandestine premarital intercourse, if discovered and proved, brings severe punishment on both man and woman; and the guilty parties are forbidden to marry for their whole lives, unless the prince by his pardon mitigates the sentence. Also both the father and mother of the household where the offence occurred suffer public disgrace for having been remiss in their duty. The reason they punish this offence so severely is that they suppose few people would join in married love – with confinement to a single partner and all the petty annoyances that married life involves – unless they were strictly restrained from promiscuity.

In choosing marriage partners they solemnly and seriously follow a custom which seemed to us foolish and absurd in the extreme. Whether she be widow or virgin, the bride-to-be is shown naked to *Not very modest,* the groom by a responsible and respectable matron; and similarly, *but not so impractical either* some respectable man presents the groom naked to his prospective

---

[81] Though in the ancient world suicide was regarded as an honourable way out of deep personal and political difficulties, neither suicide nor euthanasia was (or is) acceptable in Catholic Christianity. More discusses the 'wicked temptation' of suicide at length in *A Dialogue of Comfort against Tribulation* (1534) (*CW*, XII, 122–57).

bride. We laughed at this custom, and called it absurd; but they were just as amazed at the folly of all other peoples. When men go to buy a colt, where they are risking only a little money, they are so cautious that, though the animal is almost bare, they won't close the deal until saddle and blanket have been taken off, lest there be a hidden sore underneath.[82] Yet in the choice of a mate, which may cause either delight or disgust for the rest of their lives, men are so careless that they leave all the rest of the woman's body covered up with clothes and estimate her attractiveness from a mere handsbreadth of her person, the face, which is all they can see. And so they marry, running great risk of bitter discord, if something in either's person should offend the other. Not all people are so wise as to concern themselves solely with character; even the wise appreciate physical beauty as a supplement to a good disposition. There's no doubt that a deformity may lurk under clothing, serious enough to make a man hate his wife when it's too late to be separated from her. If some disfiguring accident takes place after marriage, each person must bear his own fate; but the Utopians think everyone should be legally protected from deception beforehand.

There is extra reason for them to be careful, because in that part of the world they are the only people who practise monogamy,[83] and *Divorce* because their marriages are seldom terminated except by death – though they do allow divorce for adultery or for intolerably offensive behaviour. A husband or wife who is an aggrieved party to such a divorce is granted leave by the senate to take a new mate, but the guilty party suffers disgrace and is permanently forbidden to remarry.[84] They absolutely forbid a husband to put away his wife

---

[82] Plato's *Laws* commends with perfect seriousness a practice similar to the Utopians': 'when people are going to live together as partners in marriage, it is vital that the fullest possible information should be available ... One should regard the prevention of mistakes here as a matter of supreme importance – so important and serious, in fact, that even the young people's recreation must be arranged with this in mind. Boys and girls must dance together at an age when plausible occasions can be found for their doing so, in order that they may have a reasonable look at each other; and they should dance naked, provided sufficient modesty and restraint are displayed by all concerned' (VI.771E–772A).

[83] In this respect the Utopians resemble the ancient Germans as portrayed by Tacitus: 'the marriage tie with them is strict: you will find nothing in their character to praise more highly. They are almost the only barbarians who are content with a wife apiece' (*Germany* 17).

[84] Although the Church in More's day permitted separation in the case of adultery, it did not allow the injured party to remarry.

against her will and without any fault on her part, just because of some bodily misfortune; they think it cruel that a person should be abandoned when most in need of comfort; and they add that old age, since it not only entails disease but is a disease itself,[85] needs more than a precarious fidelity.

It happens occasionally that a married couple cannot get along, and have both found other persons with whom they hope to live more harmoniously. After getting approval of the senate, they may then separate by mutual consent and contract new marriages. But such divorces are allowed only after the senators and their wives have carefully investigated the case. Divorce is deliberately made difficult because they know that couples will have a hard time settling down if each partner has in mind that a new relation is easily available.

They punish adulterers with the strictest form of slavery. If both parties were married, both are divorced, and the injured parties may marry one another if they want, or someone else. But if one of the injured parties continues to love such an undeserving spouse, the marriage may go on, provided the innocent person chooses to share in the labour to which every slave is condemned. And sometimes it happens that the repentance of the guilty and the devotion of the innocent party so move the prince to pity that he restores both to freedom. But a second conviction of adultery is punished by death.

No other crimes carry fixed penalties; the senate decrees a specific punishment for each misdeed, as it is considered atrocious or venial. Husbands chastise their wives and parents their children, unless the offence is so serious that public punishment is called for. Generally, the gravest crimes are punished with slavery, for they think this deters offenders just as much as immediate capital punishment, and convict labour is more beneficial to the commonwealth. Slaves, moreover, are permanent and visible reminders that crime does not pay. If the slaves rebel against their condition, then they are put instantly to death, like savage beasts which neither bars nor chains can tame. But if they are patient, they are not left altogether without hope. When subdued by long hardships, if they show by their behaviour that they regret the crime more than the punishment, their slavery is lightened or remitted altogether, sometimes by the prince's pardon, sometimes by popular vote.

Degrees of punishment left to magistrates

[85] The phrase comes from Terence's comedy *Phormio* (IV.i; l. 575).

83

The penalty for soliciting to lewdness

Attempted seduction is subject to the same penalty as seduction itself. They think that a crime attempted is as bad as one committed, and that failure should not confer advantages on a criminal who did all he could to succeed.

Pleasure derived from fools

They are very fond of fools, and think it contemptible to insult them. There is no prohibition against enjoying their foolishness, and they even regard this as beneficial to the fools. If anyone is so solemn and severe that the foolish behaviour and comic patter of a clown do not amuse him, they don't entrust him with the care of such a person, for fear that a man who gets no fun from a fool's only gift will not treat him kindly.

To deride a person for being deformed or crippled is considered disgraceful, not to the victim but to the mocker, who stupidly reproaches the cripple for something he cannot help.

Artificial beauty

Though they think it a sign of weak and sluggish character to neglect one's natural beauty, they consider cosmetics a detestable affectation. From experience they have learned that no physical attractions recommend a wife to her husband so effectually as truthfulness and honour. Though quite a few men are captured by beauty alone, none are held except by virtue and compliance.

Citizens to be animated by rewards for good conduct

The Utopians not only deter men from crime by penalties, but they incite them to virtue by public honours. Accordingly, they set up in the marketplaces statues of distinguished men who have served their country well, thinking thereby to preserve the memory of their good deeds and to spur on citizens to emulate the glory of their ancestors.

Running for office condemned

In Utopia any man who campaigns for a public office is disqualified for all of them. Their civic life is harmonious, and their public officials are never arrogant or unapproachable. They are called

Magistrates held in honour

'fathers', and that indeed is the way they behave. Because officials never extort respect from the people against their will, the people

Dignity of the ruler

respect them spontaneously, as they should. Not even the prince is distinguished from his fellow citizens by a robe or a crown; he is known only by a sheaf of grain carried before him, as the high priest is distinguished by a wax candle.[86]

Few laws

They have very few laws, and their training is such that they need no more. The chief fault they find with other nations is that, even

---

[86] Grain (suggesting prosperity) and candle (suggesting vision) symbolise the special function of each.

with infinite volumes of laws and interpretations, they cannot manage their affairs properly. They think it completely unjust to bind men by a set of laws that are too many to be read or too obscure for anyone to understand. As for lawyers, a class of men whose trade it is to manipulate cases and multiply quibbles, they wouldn't have them in the country. They think it better for each man to plead his own case, and say the same thing to the judge that he would tell his advocate. This makes for less confusion and readier access to the truth. A man speaks his mind without tricky instructions from a lawyer, and the judge examines each point carefully, taking pains to protect simple folk against the false accusations of the crafty. This sort of plain dealing is hard to find in other nations, where they have such a multitude of incomprehensibly intricate laws. But in Utopia everyone is a legal expert. For the laws are very few, as I said, and they consider the most obvious interpretation of any law to be the fairest. As they see things, all laws are promulgated for the single purpose of advising every man of his duty. Subtle interpretations admonish very few, since hardly anybody can understand them, whereas the more simple and apparent sense of the law is open to everyone. If laws are not clear, they are useless; for simple-minded men (and most men are of this sort, and must be told where their duty lies) there might as well be no laws at all as laws which can be interpreted only by devious minds after endless disputes. The common man cannot understand this legal chicanery, and couldn't even if he devoted his whole life to studying it, since he has to earn a living in the meantime.

The useless crowd of lawyers

Some free nations bordering on Utopia (the Utopians themselves previously liberated many of them from tyranny) have learned to admire the Utopian virtues, and now of their own accord ask the Utopians to supply magistrates for them. Of these magistrates, some serve for one year, others for five. When their service is over, they return home with honour and praise, while others are sent out in their place. These countries seem to have settled on an excellent scheme to safeguard their happiness and security. Since the welfare or ruin of a commonwealth depends wholly on the character of the officials, where could they make a more prudent choice than among Utopians, who cannot be tempted by money? For money is useless to them when they go home, as they soon must, and they can have no partisan or factional feelings, since they are strangers to the affairs of the city over which they rule. Wherever they take root in men's minds, these two evils, greed and faction, soon destroy all justice, which is the strongest bond of any society. The Utopians call these people who have borrowed governors from them their allies; others whom they have benefited they call simply friends.

Treaties   While other nations are constantly making, breaking and renewing treaties, the Utopians make none at all with anyone. If nature, they say, doesn't bind man adequately to his fellow man, will an alliance do so? If a man scorns nature herself, is there any reason to think he will care about mere words? They are confirmed in this view by the fact that in that part of the world, treaties and alliances between princes are not generally observed with much good faith.

In Europe, of course, and especially in these regions where the Christian faith and religion prevail, the dignity of treaties is everywhere kept sacred and inviolable. This is partly because the princes are all so just and virtuous, partly also from the awe and reverence that everyone feels for the Popes.[87] Just as the Popes themselves never promise anything that they do not scrupulously perform, so they command all other princes to abide by their promises in every way. If someone quibbles over it, by pastoral censure and sharp reproof they compel him to obey. They think, and rightly, that it would be shameful if people who are specifically called 'the faithful' acted in bad faith.

But in that new world, which is distanced from ours not so much by geography as by customs and manners, nobody trusts treaties. The greater the formalities, the more numerous and solemn the oaths, the sooner the treaty will be broken. The rulers will find some defect in the wording, which often enough they deliberately inserted themselves, so that they're never at a loss for a pretext. No treaty can be made so strong and explicit that a government will not be able to worm out of it, breaking in the process both the treaty and its own word. If such craft (not to call it deceit and fraud) were practised in private contracts, the righteous politicians would raise a

---

[87] The European rulers of the time were in fact ruthless and casual violators of treaties. So also were two recent Popes, Alexander VI and Julius II. Of the former, Machiavelli says admiringly that he 'never did anything else and never dreamed of anything else than deceiving men . . . Never was there a man more effective in swearing and who with stronger oaths confirmed a promise, but yet honored it less' (*The Prince*, chapter 18; trans. Allan Gilbert, in Niccolò Machiavelli, *The Chief Works and Others*, 3 vols. (Durham, N.C., 1958), I, 65).

great outcry against both parties, calling them sacrilegious and worthy of the gallows. Yet the very same politicians think themselves clever fellows when they give this sort of advice to kings. Thus men are apt to think that justice is a humble, plebeian virtue, far beneath the dignity of kings. Or else they conclude that there are two kinds of justice, one for the common herd, a lowly justice that creeps along the ground, hedged in everywhere and encumbered with chains; and the other, which is the justice of princes, much more free and majestic, which can do anything it wants and nothing it doesn't want.

This royal practice of keeping treaties badly is, I suppose, the reason the Utopians don't make any; doubtless if they lived here they would change their minds. However, they think it a bad idea to make treaties at all, even if they are faithfully kept. The treaty implies that men divided by some natural obstacle as slight as a hill or a brook are joined by no bond of nature; it assumes they are born rivals and enemies, and are right in trying to destroy one another except when a treaty restrains them. Besides, they see that treaties do not really promote friendship; for both parties still retain the right to prey on one another, unless extreme care has been used in drafting the treaty to outlaw freebooting. The Utopians think, on the other hand, that no man should be considered an enemy who has done no harm, that the kinship of nature is as good as a treaty, and that men are united more firmly by good will than by pacts, by their hearts than by their words.

WARFARE

They despise war as an activity fit only for beasts,[88] yet practised more by man than by any other animal. Unlike almost every other people in the world, they think nothing so inglorious as the glory won in battle. Yet on certain assigned days both men and women carry on vigorous military training, so they will be fit to fight should the need arise. They go to war only for good reasons: to protect their own land, to drive invading armies from the territories of their friends, or to liberate an oppressed people, in the name of humanity,

---

[88] A folk etymology, mistaken like most of them, derived Latin *bellum* ('war') from *belua* ('beast'). For the most part, the Utopians' attitudes towards war are similar to those of More and his humanist circle. For a full account, see R. P. Adams, *The Better Part of Valor*.

from tyranny and servitude. They war not only to protect their friends from present danger, but sometimes to avenge previous injuries; but enter a conflict only if they themselves have been consulted in advance, have approved the cause, and have demanded restitution, but in vain. Then and only then they think themselves free to declare war. They take this final step not only when their friends have been plundered, but also, and even more fiercely, when their friends' merchants have been subjected to extortion in a third country, either through laws unjust in themselves or through the perversion of good laws.

This and no other was the cause of the war which the Utopians waged a little before our time on behalf of the Nephelogetes against the Alaopolitans.[89] Under pretext of right, a wrong (as they saw it) had been inflicted on some Nephelogete traders residing in Alaopolis. Whatever the rights and wrongs of the quarrel, it developed into a fierce war, into which the neighbouring nations poured all their resources, thereby inflaming mutual hatreds. Some prosperous nations were ruined completely, others badly shaken. One trouble led to another, and in the end the Nephelogetes not only crushed the Alaopolitans but (since the Utopians weren't involved on their own account) reduced them to slavery – even though before the war the victors had not been remotely comparable in power to their rivals.

So sharply do the Utopians punish wrong done to their friends, even in matters of mere money; but they are not so strict in enforcing their own rights. When they are cheated in any way, so long as no bodily harm is done, their anger goes no further than cutting off trade relations with that nation till restitution is made. The reason is not that they care less for their own citizens than for their friends', but that the latter, when they lose goods from their private stock, feel the loss more bitterly. The Utopian traders, by contrast, lose nothing but what belongs to the general public, more particularly goods that were already abundant at home, even superfluous, since otherwise they wouldn't have been exported. Hence no one individual has to stand the loss. So small an injury, which affects neither the life nor the livelihood of any of their own people, they consider it cruel to avenge by the deaths of many soldiers. On the other hand, if one of their own is maimed or killed anywhere, whether by a public

[89] More Greek compounds: 'People Born from the Clouds' and 'People without a Country'.

official or by a private citizen, they first send envoys to look into the circumstances; then they demand that the guilty persons be surrendered; and if that demand is refused, they are not to be put off, but at once declare war. If the guilty persons are surrendered, their punishment is death or slavery.

The Utopians are not only troubled but ashamed when their forces gain a bloody victory, thinking it folly to pay too high a price even for the best goods. But if they overcome the enemy by skill and cunning, they exult mightily, celebrate a public triumph, and raise a monument as for a glorious exploit. They think they have really acted with manly virtue when they have won a victory such as no animal except man could have achieved – a victory gained by strength of understanding. Bears, lions, boars, wolves, dogs and other wild beasts fight with their bodies, they say; and most of them are superior to us in strength and ferocity; but we outdo them all in shrewdness and rationality. *Victory too dearly bought*

The only thing they aim at, in going to war, is to secure what would have prevented the declaration of war, if the enemy had conceded it beforehand. Or, if they cannot get that, they try to take such bitter revenge on those who provoked them that they will be afraid ever to do it again. These are their chief aims, which they prosecute vigorously, yet in such a way as to avoid danger, rather than to win fame or glory.

As soon as war is declared, therefore, they have their secret agents set up overnight many placards, each marked with their official seal, in the most conspicuous places throughout enemy territory. In these proclamations they promise immense rewards to anyone who will eliminate the enemy's king. They offer smaller but still substantial sums for killing any of a list of other individuals whom they name. These are the persons whom they regard as most responsible, after the king, for plotting aggression against them. The reward for an assassin is doubled for anyone who succeeds in bringing in one of the proscribed men alive. The same reward, plus a guarantee of personal safety, is offered to any one of the proscribed men who turns against his comrades. As a result, the enemies of the Utopians quickly come to suspect everyone, particularly one another; and the many perils of their situation lead to panic. They know very well that many of them, including especially their princes, have been betrayed by those in whom they placed complete trust – so effective are bribes as an incitement to crime. Knowing this, the Utopians are lavish in their promises of bounty. Being well aware of the risks their agents must run, they make sure the payments are in proportion to the peril; thus they not only offer, but actually deliver, enormous sums of gold, as well as valuable landed estates in very secure locations on the territory of their friends.

Other nations condemn this custom of bidding for and buying the life of an enemy as the cruel villainy of a degenerate mind; but the Utopians consider it good policy, both wise and merciful. It enables them to win tremendous wars without fighting any actual battles; and it enables them, by the sacrifice of a few guilty men, to spare the lives of many innocent persons who would have died in the fighting, some on their side, some on the enemy's. They pity the mass of the enemy's soldiers almost as much as their own citizens, for they know common people do not go to war of their own accord, but are driven to it by the passions of their rulers.

If assassination does not work, they stir up dissensions in enemy ranks by inciting the king's brother or some other member of the nobility to plot for the crown.[90] If internal discord dies down, they try to rouse up neighbouring peoples against the enemy, by reviving forgotten claims to dominion, of which kings always have an ample supply.

When they promise their resources to help in a war, they send money very freely, but commit their soldiers very sparingly indeed. They hold their own people dear, and value them so highly that they would not exchange one of their citizens for an enemy's king. But gold and silver, which they keep for the purpose of war alone, they spend without hesitation; after all, they will continue to live just as well even if they waste the whole sum. Besides the wealth they have at home, they keep a vast treasure abroad since, as I described before, many nations owe them money. So they hire mercenary soldiers from all sides, especially the Zapoletes.[91]

[90] The stratagems of this paragraph, presented without criticism, compare interestingly with the recommendations of the corrupt privy councillors in Hythloday's imaginary strategy session (p. 30).

[91] As the gloss points out, the Zapoletes (from Greek: 'busy sellers') resemble the Swiss, who provided Europe's most feared and hated mercenaries. Many Italian princes, as well as the French, hired Swiss mercenaries; and Popes have Swiss guards to this day. Johann Froben, who printed the 1518 editions of *Utopia*, was Swiss himself and omitted the gloss.

These people live five hundred miles to the east of Utopia, and are rough, rude and fierce. The forests and mountains where they are bred are the kind of country they like: tough and rugged. They are a hard race, capable of standing heat, cold and drudgery, unacquainted with any luxuries, careless of the houses they live in or the clothes they wear; they don't till the fields but raise cattle instead. Most survive by hunting and stealing. These people are born for battle and are always spoiling for a fight; they seek it out at every opportunity. Leaving their own country in great numbers, they offer themselves for cheap hire to anyone in need of warriors. The only art they know for earning a living is the art of taking life. *A people not so unlike the Swiss*

For the people who pay them they fight with great courage and complete loyalty, but they will not bind themselves to serve for any fixed period of time. If someone, even the enemy, offers them more money tomorrow, they will take his side; and the day after tomorrow, if a trifle more is offered to bring them back, they'll return to their first employers. Hardly a war is fought in which a good number of them are not engaged on both sides. It happens every day that men who are united by ties of blood and have served together in friendship through long campaigns, but who are now separated into opposing armies, meet in battle. Forgetful of kinship and comradeship alike, they furiously run one another through, for no other reason than that they were hired for paltry pay by opposing kings. They care so much for money that they can easily be induced to change sides for an increase of only a penny a day. They have picked up the habit of avarice, but none of the profit; for what they earn by bloodletting they quickly squander on debauchery of the most squalid sort.

Because the Utopians pay better than anyone else, these people are ready to serve them against any enemy whatever. And the Utopians, as they seek out the best possible men for proper uses, hire these, the worst possible men, for improper uses. When the situation requires, they thrust the Zapoletes into the positions of greatest danger by offering them immense rewards. Most of these bravos never come back to collect their stipend, but the Utopians faithfully pay off those who do survive, to encourage them to try it again. As for how many Zapoletes get killed, the Utopians never worry about that, for they think they would deserve well of all mankind if they could exterminate from the face of the earth that entire vicious and disgusting race.[92]

After the Zapoletes, they employ as auxiliaries the soldiers of the people for whom they have taken up arms, and then squadrons of all their other friends. Last, they add their own citizens, including some man of known bravery to command the entire army. They also appoint two substitutes for him, who hold no rank as long as he is safe. But if the commander is captured or killed, the first of these two substitutes becomes his successor, and in case of a mishap to him, the other.[93] Thus, despite the many accidents of war, they ensure that the whole army will not be disorganised through loss of the general.

Only volunteers are sent to fight abroad; they are picked men from within each city. No one is forced to fight abroad against his will, because they think a man who is naturally fearful will act weakly at best, and may even spread panic among his comrades. But if their own country is invaded they call to arms even the fearful (as long as they are physically fit), placing them on shipboard among braver men, or here and there along fortifications, where there is no place to run away. Thus shame at failing their countrymen, desperation at the immediate presence of the enemy and the impossibility of flight often combine to overcome their fear, and they turn brave out of sheer necessity.

Just as no man is forced into a foreign war against his will, so women are allowed to accompany their men on military service if they want to – not only not forbidden, but encouraged and praised for doing so. Each leaves with her husband, and they stand shoulder to shoulder in the line of battle; in addition, they place around a man all of his children, kinsmen and blood- or marriage-relations, so that those who by nature have most reason to help one another may be closest at hand for mutual support. It is a matter of great reproach for either spouse to come home without the other, or for a son to

---

[92] Sixteenth-century accounts of horrors perpetrated by mercenaries – including an account by More of the sacking of Rome in 1527 (*Dialogue Concerning Heresies*, *CW*, VI, 370–2) – help to explain the Utopians' genocidal policy towards the Zapoletes. In *The Education of a Christian Prince*, Erasmus says of mercenaries that 'there is no class of men more abject and indeed more damnable' (*CWE*, XXVII, 283). How the Utopians reconcile their employment of the Zapoletes with their aim of minimising bloodshed and plunder in war is unclear.

[93] This is a Spartan practice. See Thucydides, *The Peloponnesian War* IV.xxxviii.

return after losing his father. The result is that as long as the enemy stands his ground, the hand-to-hand fighting is apt to be long and bitter, ending only when everyone is dead.

As I observed, they take every precaution to avoid fighting in person, so long as they can use mercenaries to fight for them. But when they are forced to enter the battle, they are as bold in the struggle as they were formerly prudent in putting it off. In the first charge they are not fierce, but gradually as the fighting goes on they grow more determined, putting up a steady, stubborn resistance. Their spirit is so strong that they will die rather than yield ground. They have no anxieties about making a living at home, nor any worry about the future of their families (and that sort of care often daunts the boldest spirits); so their spirit is proud and unconquerable. Knowing the job of warfare and knowing it well gives them extra confidence; also they have been trained from infancy in sound principles of conduct (which their education and the good institutions of their society both reinforce); and that too adds to their courage. They don't hold life so cheap that they throw it away recklessly, nor so dear that they grasp it greedily at the price of shame when duty bids them give it up.

At the height of the battle, a band of the bravest young men who have taken a special oath devote themselves to seeking out the opposing general. They assail him directly, they lay secret traps for him, they hit at him from near and far. A continuous stream of fresh men keep up the assault as the exhausted drop out. In the end, they rarely fail to kill or capture him, unless he takes flight.

The enemy general to be most fiercely attacked, so as to end the war sooner

When they win a battle, it never ends in a massacre, for they would much rather take prisoners than cut throats. They never pursue fugitives without keeping one line of their army drawn up under the colours and ready to renew the fight. They are so careful of this that if they win the victory with this last reserve force (after the rest of their army has been beaten), they would rather let the enemy army escape than get into the way of pursuing fugitives with their own ranks in disorder. They recall what has happened more than once to themselves: that when the enemy seemed to have the best of the day, had routed the main Utopian force, and scattered to round up runaways, a few Utopians held in reserve and watching their opportunity have suddenly attacked the dispersed enemy just when he felt safe and had lowered his guard. Thereby they changed the fortune of the day, snatched certain victory out of the enemy's hands, and, though beaten themselves, were able to overcome their conquerors.

It is not easy to say whether they are more crafty in laying ambushes or more clever in avoiding those laid for them. Sometimes they seem about to run away when that is the last thing in their minds; when they are really ready to retreat, you would never guess it. If they are too few to mount an attack, or if the terrain is unsuitable, they shift their ground silently by night or get away by some stratagem; or if they have to withdraw by day, they do so gradually, and in such good order that they are as dangerous to attack then as if they were advancing. They fortify their camps thoroughly, with a deep, broad ditch all around them, the earth being thrown inward to form a wall; the work is done not by labourers but by the soldiers themselves with their own hands. The whole army pitches in, except for a guard posted around the workers to prevent surprise attack. With so many hands at work, they complete great fortifications, enclosing wide areas with unbelievable speed.

The variety of their weapons Their armour is strong enough for protection, but does not prevent free movement of the body; indeed, it doesn't even interfere with swimming, and part of their training consists of swimming in armour. For long-range fighting they use arrows, which they fire with great force and accuracy, from horseback as well as on the ground. At close quarters they use not swords but battle-axes, which because of their sharp edge and great weight are lethal weapons, whether used to slash or thrust. They are very skilful in inventing machines of war, but carefully conceal them, since if they were made known before they were needed, the enemy might turn them to ridicule and lessen their effect. Their first consideration in designing them is to make them easy to carry and aim.[94]

Truces Truces made with the enemy they observe religiously and will not break even if provoked. They do not ravage the enemy's territory or burn his crops; indeed, so far as possible, they avoid any trampling of the fields by men or horses, thinking they may need the grain

---

[94] The military devices of the Utopians are a patchwork of different notions from the common knowledge of the day. Their camps are fortified like Roman ones. Their reliance on archery links them with the English – though their skill in shooting arrows from horseback recalls the ancient Parthians and Scythians. The 'machines' are evidently like Roman *ballistae, arietes, scorpiones* (stone-throwers, battering rams, dart-hurlers); but the emphasis on their portability probably reflects contemporary experience with cannon, which were terribly hard to drag over the muddy routes of the time.

themselves. Unless he is a spy, they injure no unarmed man. Cities that are surrendered to them they keep intact; even after storming a place, they do not plunder it, but put to death the men who prevented surrender, enslave the other defenders, and do no harm to civilians. If they find any inhabitants who recommended surrender, they give them a share in the property of the condemned. What is left they divide among their auxiliaries; for themselves, the Utopians never take any booty.

After a war is ended they collect the cost of it, not from the allies for whose sake they undertook it, but from the conquered. They take as indemnity not only money, which they set aside to finance future wars, but also landed estates, from which they may enjoy forever a substantial annual income. They now have property of this sort in many different countries, acquired on many occasions and augmented over the years in various ways, till its revenue amounts to over seven hundred thousand ducats a year.[95] As managers of these estates, they send abroad some of their citizens with the title of Financial Factors. Though they live on the properties in great style and conduct themselves like magnates, plenty of income is still left over to be put in the treasury, unless they lend it to the conquered nation. They often do the latter until they happen to need the money, and even then it's rare for them to call in the entire debt. As I've already noted, they also give some of the estates to those who have taken great risks on their behalf.

But today the victors foot most of the bill

If a foreign prince takes up arms and prepares to invade their land, they immediately attack him full force outside their own borders. For they don't like to wage war on their own soil, and would not allow foreign auxiliaries on their island under any necessity.

RELIGIONS OF THE UTOPIANS

There are different forms of religion throughout the island, and in the different cities as well. Some worship as a god the sun, others the moon, still others one of the planets. There are some who worship a man of past ages, conspicuous either for virtue or glory; they consider him not only a god, but the supreme god. The vast majority of

---

[95] Gold coins of this name were minted by several European countries. Four ducats of Burgundy, Venice or Hungary were roughly equivalent to an English pound; and the pound itself was worth several hundred times its value today.

Utopians, however, and among these all the wisest, believe nothing
of the sort: they believe in a single power, unknown, eternal, infinite, inexplicable, far beyond the grasp of the human mind, and diffused throughout the universe, not physically, but in influence.
Him they call father, and to him alone they attribute the origin,
increase, progress, change and end of all visible things; they do not
offer divine honours to any other.

Though the other sects differ from this group in various particular doctrines, they all agree in a single main head, that there is one
supreme power, the maker and ruler of the universe; in their native
tongue they all call him Mithra.[96] Different people define him differently, and each supposes the object of his worship is the special
vessel of that great force which all people agree in worshipping. But
gradually they are coming to forsake this mixture of superstitions
and unite in that one religion which seems more reasonable than any
of the others. And there is no doubt that the other religions would
have disappeared long ago, had not various unlucky accidents,
befalling certain Utopians who were thinking of changing their religion, been interpreted as a sign of divine anger, not chance – as if the
deity who was being abandoned were avenging an insult against
himself.

But after they heard from us the name of Christ, and learned of
his teachings, his life, his miracles, and the no less marvellous
devotion of the many martyrs whose blood, freely shed, had drawn
nations far and near into the Christian fellowship, you would not
believe how they were impressed. Either through the secret inspi-
ration of God, or because Christianity seemed very like the belief
that most prevails among them, they were well disposed towards it
from the start. But I think they were also much influenced by the fact
that Christ encouraged his disciples to practise community of
Monasteries goods, and that among the truest groups of Christians, the practice
still prevails.[97] Whatever the reason, no small number of them
chose to join our communion and were washed in the holy water of
baptism.

[96] In ancient Persian religion, Mithra or Mithras, the spirit of light, was the supreme
force of good in the universe. Recall that the Utopians' language 'resembles Persian in
most respects' (p. 78), and that under the name of Mithra some of them worship the sun
or other heavenly bodies.

[97] The communist practice of the disciples is described in Acts 2:44–5 and 4:32–5.

By that time, two of our group had died, and among us four survivors there was, I am sorry to say, no priest. So, though they received instruction in other matters, they still lack those sacraments which in our religion can be administered only by priests.[98] They do, however, understand what these are, and eagerly desire them. In fact, they dispute warmly whether a man chosen from among themselves could be considered a priest without ordination by a Christian bishop. Though they seemed about to select such a person, they had not yet done so when I left.

Those who have not accepted Christianity make no effort to restrain others from it, nor do they criticise new converts to it. While I was there, only one of the Christians got into trouble with the law. As soon as he was baptised, he took on himself to preach the Christian religion publicly, with more zeal than discretion. We warned him not to do so, but he soon worked himself up to a pitch where he not only preferred our religion, but condemned all others as profane, leading their impious and sacrilegious followers to the hell-fires they richly deserved. After he had been going on in this style for a long time, they arrested him. He was tried on a charge, not of despising their religion, but of creating a public disorder, convicted, and sentenced to exile. For it is one of their oldest rules that no one should suffer for his religion.

Men must be drawn to religion by its merits

Even before he took over the island, King Utopus had heard that the natives were continually squabbling over religious matters. Actually, he found it easy to conquer the country because the different sects were too busy fighting one another to oppose him. As soon as he had gained the victory, therefore, he decreed that every man might cultivate the religion of his choice, and proselytise for it too, provided he did so quietly, modestly, rationally and without bitterness towards others. If persuasions failed, no man might resort to abuse or violence, under penalty of exile or slavery.

Utopus laid down these rules not simply for the sake of peace, which he saw was being destroyed by constant quarrels and implacable hatreds, but also for the sake of religion itself. In such matters he was not at all quick to dogmatise, because he suspected that God perhaps likes various forms of worship and has therefore deliber-

---

[98] The Catholic Church allows that, in case of need, any person can perform baptism. The other six sacraments require an ordained priest.

ately inspired different men with different views. On the other hand, he was quite sure that it was arrogant folly for anyone to enforce conformity with his own beliefs by threats or violence.[99] He supposed that if one religion is really true and the rest are false, the true one will sooner or later prevail by its own natural strength, if men will only consider the matter reasonably and moderately. But if they try to decide things by fighting and rioting, since the worst men are always the most headstrong, the best and holiest religion in the world will be crowded out by foolish superstitions, like grain choked out of a field by thorns and briars. So he left the whole matter open, allowing each person to choose what he would believe. The only exception was a positive and strict law against anyone who should sink so far below the dignity of human nature as to think that the soul perishes with the body, or that the universe is ruled by blind chance, not divine providence.[100]

Thus they believe that after this life vices will be punished and virtue rewarded. Anyone who denies this proposition they consider less than a man, since he has degraded the sublimity of his own soul to the base level of a beast's wretched body. Still less will they count him as one of their citizens, since he would openly despise all the laws and customs of society, if not prevented by fear. Who can doubt that a man who has nothing to fear but the law, and no hope of life beyond the grave, will do anything he can to evade his country's laws by craft or to break them by violence, in order to gratify his own personal greed? Therefore a man who holds such views is offered no honours, entrusted with no offices, and given no public responsibility; he is universally regarded as a low and sordid fellow. Yet they do not punish him, because they are persuaded that no man can choose to believe by a mere act of the will. They do not compel him by

[99] This was not the attitude More took a decade later, when he was involved in the prosecution of Protestants. In the *Dialogue Concerning Heresies*, he wrote that 'if it were now doubtful and ambiguous whether the church of Christ were in the right rule of doctrine or not, then were it very necessary to give them all good audience that could and would anything dispute on either party for or against it, to the end that if we were now in a wrong way, we might leave it and walk in some better' (*CW*, VI, 345–6). In Utopia, which has not had the Christian revelation, a high degree of religious toleration is appropriate; in England, the fact that the 'right rule of doctrine' was clearly established justified, so More believed, harsh suppression of dissenting views.

[100] The Utopians regard basic truths about immortality and divine providence as attainable by natural reason and as providing the only rational sanction for the life of virtue (pp. 68–9).

threats to dissemble his views, nor do they tolerate in the matter any deceit or lying, which they detest as next door to deliberate malice. The man may not argue with common people on behalf of his opinion; but in the presence of priests and other important persons, they not only permit but encourage it. For they are confident that in the end his madness will yield to reason.

There are some others, in fact no small number of them, who err the other way in supposing that animals have immortal souls, though not comparable to ours in excellence nor destined to equal felicity. These men are not thought to be evil, their opinion is not considered wholly unreasonable, and so they are not interfered with.

A strange opinion on the souls of animals

Almost all the Utopians are absolutely convinced that man's bliss after death will be enormous and eternal; thus they lament every man's sickness, but mourn over a death only if the man was torn from life wretchedly and against his will. Such behaviour they take to be a very bad sign, as if the soul, despairing and conscious of guilt, dreaded death through a secret premonition of punishments to come. Besides, they suppose God can hardly be well pleased with the coming of one who, when he is summoned, does not come gladly, but is dragged off reluctantly and against his will. Such a death fills the onlookers with horror, and they carry off the corpse to the cemetery in melancholy silence. There, after begging God to have mercy on his spirit and to pardon his infirmities, they bury the unhappy man. But when someone dies blithely and full of good hope, they do not mourn for him, but carry the body cheerfully away, singing and commending the dead man's soul to God. They cremate[101] him in a spirit of reverence more than of grief, and erect a tombstone on which the dead man's honours are inscribed. As they go home, they talk of his character and deeds, and no part of his life is mentioned more frequently or more gladly than his joyful death.

They think that recollecting the good qualities of a man inspires the living to behave virtuously and is the most acceptable form of honour to the dead. For they think that dead persons are actually present among us, and hear what we say about them, though through the dullness of human sight they remain invisible. Given

---

[101] Cremation was standard practice in most of the ancient world, but was not used by Christians before the nineteenth century because it was thought to be at odds with the doctrine of resurrection of the body.

their state of bliss, the dead must be able to travel freely where they please, and it would be unkind of them to cast off every desire of seeing those friends to whom in life they had been joined by mutual affection and charity. Like other good qualities they think that after death charity is increased rather than diminished in all good men; and thus they believe the dead come frequently among the living, to observe their words and acts.[102] Hence they go about their business the more confidently because of their trust in such protectors; and the belief that their forefathers are physically present keeps men from any secret dishonourable deed.

Fortune-telling and other vain, superstitious divinations, such as other peoples take very seriously, they consider ridiculous and contemptible. But they venerate miracles which occur without the help of nature, considering them direct and visible manifestations of the divinity. Indeed, they report that miracles have often occurred in their country. Sometimes in great and dangerous crises they pray publicly for a miracle, which they then anticipate with great confidence, and obtain.

They think the investigation of nature and the reverence arising from it are most acceptable to God. There are some people, however, and quite a few of them, who from religious motives reject *The active life* literary and scientific pursuits, and refuse all leisure, but devote their full time to good works. Only by constant dedication to the offices of charity, these people think, can happiness after death be earned; and so they are always busy. Some tend the sick; others repair roads, clean ditches, rebuild bridges, dig turf, sand, or stones; still others fell trees and cut them up, and transport wood, grain or other commodities into the cities by wagon. They work for private citizens as well as for the public, and work even harder than slaves. With cheery good will they undertake any task that is so rough, hard and dirty that most people refuse to tackle it because of the toil, tedium and frustration involved. While constantly engaged in heavy labour themselves, they procure leisure for others, yet claim no credit for it. They neither criticise the way others live, nor

---

[102] In the *Dialogue Concerning Heresies*, More wrote of the saints that 'if their holy souls live, there will no wise man ween them worse, and of less love and charity to men that need their help, when they be now in heaven, than they had when they were here in earth ... When saints were in this world at liberty and might walk the world about, ween we that in heaven they stand tied to a post?' (*CW*, VI, 211, 213).

boast of their own doings. The more they put themselves in the position of slaves, the more highly they are honoured by everyone.

These people are of two sects. The first are celibates who abstain not only from sex, but also from eating meat, and some from any sort of animal food whatever. They reject all the pleasures of this life as harmful, and look forward only to the joys of the life to come, which they hope to merit by hard labour and all-night vigils. As they hope to attain it soon, they are cheerful and active in the here and now. The other kind are just as fond of hard work, but prefer to marry. They don't despise the comforts of marriage, but think as they owe nature their labour, so they owe children to their country. Unless it interferes with their labour, they avoid no pleasure, and gladly eat meat, precisely because they think it makes them stronger for any sort of heavy work. The Utopians regard the second sort as more sensible, but the first sort as holier. If anyone chose celibacy over marriage and a hard life over a comfortable one on grounds of reason alone, they would laugh at him; but as these men say they are motivated by religion, the Utopians respect and revere them. On no subject are they warier of jumping to conclusions than in this matter of religion. Such, then, are the men whom in their own language they call Buthrescas, a term which can be translated as 'specially religious'.[103]

Their priests are of great holiness and therefore very few. In each city there are no more than thirteen, one for each church. In case of war, seven of them go out with the army, and seven substitutes are appointed to fill their places for the time being. When the regular priests come back, the substitutes return to their former posts, serving as assistants to the high priest until one of the regular thirteen dies, when a substitute takes his place. The high priest is, of course, in authority over all the others. Like all other officials, priests are elected by secret popular vote, to avoid partisan feeling.[104] After election they are ordained by the college of priests.

They preside over divine worship, decree religious rites, and act as censors of public morality; for a man to be summoned before them and scolded for not living an honourable life is considered a

---

[103] 'Buthrescas' is another Greek compound, translated in the text. The constant, selfless industry of the Buthrescas embodies the monastic ideal.

[104] They are elected from the class of scholars – whose members are nominated by the priests and elected by the syphogrants (p. 53).

great disgrace. As the duty of the priests is merely to counsel and advise, so correcting and punishing offenders is the duty of the prince and other officials, though the priests may and do exclude flagrant sinners from divine service. Hardly any punishment is more dreaded than this; the excommunicate incurs great infamy, and is tortured by the fear of damnation. Not even his body is altogether secure, for unless he quickly convinces the priests of his repentance, he will be seized and punished by the senate for impiety.

The priests do the teaching of children and young people.[105] Instruction in good manners and pure morals is considered no less important than learning proper. From the first they make every effort to instil in the pupils' minds, while they are still young and tender, principles useful to the community. What is planted in the minds of children lives on in the minds of adults and serves to strengthen the commonwealth; its decline can always be traced to vices which arise from wrong attitudes.

Female priests   Women are not debarred from the priesthood, but only a widow of advanced years is ever chosen, and it doesn't happen often. Except for women who are priests themselves, the wives of priests are the most important women in the whole country.

No official is more honoured among the Utopians than the priest, to such an extent that even if one of them commits a crime, he is not *Unworthy priests* brought to court, but left to God and his own conscience. They think it wrong to lay human hands on a man, however guilty, who has been specially consecrated to God, as a holy offering, so to speak. This custom is the easier for them to observe because their priests are so few and so carefully selected. Besides, it rarely happens that a man chosen for his goodness and raised to high dignities solely because of his moral character will fall into corruption and vice. If such a thing should happen, human nature being as changeable as it is, no great harm is to be feared, because the priests are so few and have no power beyond that which derives from their good *But what a crowd* repute. In fact, the reason for having so few priests is to prevent the *of them we have!* order, now so highly esteemed, from being cheapened by numbers. Besides, they think it would be hard to find many men qualified for a dignity to which merely ordinary virtues could never raise them.

---

[105] Surely the priests only supervise the teaching. There are but thirteen of them per city, whereas each city includes a good many thousand children.

Their priests are esteemed no less highly abroad than at home, the reason for which can be seen, I think, from the following account. Whenever their armies join in battle, the Utopian priests are to be found, a little removed from the fray but not far, wearing their sacred vestments and down on their knees. With hands raised to heaven, they pray first of all for peace, and then for victory to their own side, but without much bloodshed on either part. Should their side be victorious, they rush among the combatants and restrain the rage of their own men against the defeated. If any of the enemy see these priests and call to them, it is enough to save their lives; to touch the flowing robes of a priest will save all their property from confiscation. This custom has brought them such veneration among all peoples, and given them such genuine authority, that they have saved Utopians from the rage of the enemy as often as they have protected the enemy from Utopians. Sometimes when the Utopian line has buckled, when the field was lost, and the enemy was rushing in to kill and plunder, the priests have intervened, separated the armies, and concluded an equitable peace. There was never anywhere a tribe so fierce, cruel and barbarous as not to hold their persons sacrosanct and inviolable.

O priests far more holy than our own!

The Utopians celebrate the first and last days of every month, and likewise of each year, as holy days. They divide the year into months, which they measure by the orbit of the moon, just as they measure the year itself by the course of the sun. In their language, the first days are known as the Cynemern and the last days as the Trapemern, which is to say 'First-feast' and 'Last-feast'.[106] Their churches are beautifully constructed, finely adorned, and large enough to hold a great many worshippers. This is a necessity, since churches are so few.[107] Their interiors are all rather dark, not from architectural ignorance, but from deliberate policy; for the priests

Holidays observed by the Utopians

What their churches are like

[106] More Greek compounds, literally meaning 'Dog-day' (or possibly 'Starting-day') and 'Turning-day'. A note in J. H. Lupton's edition of *Utopia* explains that in ancient Greece the 'dog's day' was 'strictly the night between the old and new [months], when food was placed out at the cross-roads, and the barking of the dogs was taken as a sign of the approach of Hecate [goddess of darkness and the underworld].' It may be relevant that Solon, the legendary lawgiver of Athens, called the last day of each month the 'Old-and-New day' (Diogenes Laertius 1.58).

[107] Doubtless there are several shifts of worship, but even so the churches must be *very* large: there are thirteen of them in each city, and each city contains over 100,000 people.

(they say) think that in bright light the congregation's thoughts will go wandering, whereas a dim light concentrates the mind and aids devotion.

Though there are various religions in Utopia, as I've said, all of them, even the most diverse, agree in the main point, which is worship of the divine nature; they are like travellers going to a single destination by different roads. So nothing is seen or heard in the churches that does not square with all the creeds. If any sect has a special rite of its own, that is celebrated in a private house; the public service is ordered by a ritual which in no way derogates from any of the private services. Therefore in the churches no images of the gods are seen, so that each man may be free to form his own image of God after his heart's desire, in any shape he pleases.[108] There is no special name for God, apart from the common word Mithra. Whatever the nature of the divine majesty may be, they agree to refer to it by that single word, and their prayers are so phrased as to accommodate the beliefs of all the different sects.

They meet in their churches, therefore, on the evening of 'Last-feast', and while still fasting they thank God for their prosperity during the month or year just ending. Next day, which is 'First-feast', they all flock to the churches in the morning to pray for prosperity and happiness in the month or year just beginning. On the day *The Utopian* of 'Last-feast', at home, before they go to church, wives kneel before *confession* their husbands and children before their parents, to confess their various failings and acts of negligence, and beg forgiveness for their offences. Thus if any cloud of anger or resentment has arisen in the family, it is dispersed, and they can attend divine services with clear *But among us the* and untroubled minds, for they are too scrupulous to worship with a *worst sinners try to* rankling conscience.[109] If they are aware of hatred or anger towards *crowd closest to the* *altar* anyone, they do not take part in divine services till they have been

---

[108] In one way or another, Utopian religion answers or somehow satisfies a great many of the complaints of the religious reformers of More's time – including complaints about idolatry and superstitious practices, ecclesiastical wealth and corruption, and censorship of expression on religious matters.

[109] Cf. Christ's injunction: 'if thou bring thy gift to the altar, and there rememberest that thy brother hath ought against thee; Leave there thy gift before the altar, and go thy way; first be reconciled to thy brother, and then come and offer thy gift' (Matthew 5:23–4). The Catholic institution of confession to priests is evidently not paralleled in Utopia. More pointed out to his daughter Margaret that 'in Greece before Christ's days they used not confession, no more the men then, than the beasts now' (*The Correspondence of Sir Thomas More*, ed. Elizabeth F. Rogers (Princeton, 1947), p. 520).

reconciled and have cleansed their hearts, for fear of some swift and terrible punishment.

As they enter the church they separate, men going to the right side and women to the left.[110] Then they take their seats so that the males of each household are placed in front of the head of that household, while the womenfolk are directly in front of the mother of the family. In this way they ensure that everyone's public behaviour is supervised by the same person whose authority and discipline direct him at home. They take great care that the young are everywhere placed in the company of their elders. For if children were trusted to the care of other children, they might spend in infantile foolery the time they should devote to developing a religious fear of the gods, which is the greatest and almost the only incitement to virtue.

They slaughter no animals in their sacrifices, and do not think that a merciful God, who gave life to all creatures that they might live, will be gratified with the shedding of blood. They burn incense, scatter perfumes and light a great number of candles – not that they think these practices profit the divine nature in any way, any more than human prayers do; but they like this harmless kind of worship. They feel that sweet smells, lights and rituals somehow elevate the mind and lift it with a livelier devotion towards the adoration of God. When they go to church the people all wear white. The priest wears a robe of many colours, wonderful for its workmanship and decoration, though not of materials as costly as one would suppose. It contains no gold embroidery nor any precious stones, but is decorated with the feathers of different birds so skilfully woven together that the value of the handiwork far exceeds the cost of the richest materials.[111] Also, certain symbolic mysteries are hidden in the patterning of the feathers on the robes, the meaning of which is carefully handed down among the priests. These messages serve to remind them of God's benefits towards them, and consequently of the gratitude they owe to God, as well as of their duty to one another.

As the priest in his robes appears from the vestry, the people all fall to the ground in reverence. The stillness is so complete that the

---

[110] Separation of the sexes in church had been customary since the early Christian centuries.

[111] The choice of feathers for the vestments may reflect Vespucci's observation that the Indians' riches 'consist of variegated birds' feathers' (*Four Voyages*, p. 98).

Utopian music

scene strikes one with awe, as if a divinity were actually present. After remaining in this posture for some time, they rise at a word from the priest. Then they sing hymns to the accompaniment of musical instruments, quite different in shape from those in our part of the world. Many of them produce sweeter tones than ours, but others are not even comparable. In one respect, however, they are beyond doubt far ahead of us, because all their music, both vocal and instrumental, renders and expresses natural feelings and perfectly matches the sound to the subject.[112] Whether the words of the psalm are cheerful, supplicatory, serene, troubled, mournful, or angry, the music represents the meaning through the melody so admirably that it penetrates and inspires the minds of the ardent hearers. Finally, the priest and the people together recite certain fixed forms of prayer, so composed that what they all repeat in unison each individual can apply to himself.

In these prayers the worshippers acknowledge God to be the creator and ruler of the universe and the author of all good things. They thank God for benefits received, and particularly for the divine favour which placed them in the happiest of commonwealths and inspired them with religious ideas which they hope are the truest. If they are wrong in this, and if there is some sort of society or religion more acceptable to God than the present one, they pray that he will, in his goodness, reveal it to them, for they are ready to follow wherever he leads. But if their form of society is the best and their religion the truest, then they pray that God will keep them steadfast, and bring other mortals to the same way of life and the same religious faith – unless, indeed, there is something in this variety of religions which delights his inscrutable will.

Then they pray that after an easy death God will receive each of them to himself, how soon or late it is not for them to say. But if it please God's divine majesty, they ask to be brought to him soon, even by the hardest possible death, rather than be kept away from him longer, even by the most prosperous of earthly careers. When this prayer has been said, they prostrate themselves on the ground again; then after a little while they rise and go to dinner. The rest of the day they pass in games and military training.

---

[112] Surtz points out that Hythloday's dissatisfaction with the increasingly elaborate church music of his time was shared by many other intellectuals (*CW*, IV, 555–6).

Now I have described to you as accurately as I could the structure of that commonwealth which I consider not only the best but indeed the only one that can rightfully claim that name. In other places men talk very liberally of the commonwealth, but what they mean is simply their own wealth; in Utopia, where there is no private business, every man zealously pursues the public business. And in both places men are right to act as they do. For elsewhere, even though the commonwealth may flourish, each man knows that unless he makes separate provision for himself, he may perfectly well die of hunger. Bitter necessity, then, forces men to look out for themselves rather than for the people, that is, for other people. But in Utopia, where everything belongs to everybody, no man need fear that, so long as the public warehouses are filled, he will ever lack for anything he needs. Distribution is not one of their problems; in Utopia no men are poor, no men are beggars, and though no man owns anything, everyone is rich.

For what can be greater riches than for a man to live joyfully and peacefully, free from all anxieties, and without worries about making a living? No man is bothered by his wife's querulous complaints about money, no man fears poverty for his son, or struggles to scrape up a dowry for his daughter. Each man can feel secure of his own livelihood and happiness, and of his whole family's as well: wife, sons, grandsons, great-grandsons, great-great-grandsons, and that whole long line of descendants that the gentry are so fond of contemplating. Indeed, even those who once worked but can no longer do so are cared for just as well as if they were still productive.

At this point, I'd like to see anyone venture to compare this equity of the Utopians with the so-called justice that prevails among other nations – among whom let me perish if I can discover the slightest scrap of justice or fairness. What kind of justice is it when a nobleman, a goldsmith,[113] a moneylender, or someone else who makes his living by doing either nothing at all or something completely useless to the commonwealth, gets to live a life of luxury and grandeur, while in the meantime a labourer, a carter, a carpenter, or a farmer

---

[113] In addition to being the creators of objects which are, from the Utopian point of view, worthless, goldsmiths often functioned as bankers. As the inclusion of moneylenders in this list suggests, the idea that lending money at interest constituted sinful usury remained strong in More's time – though the sentence also makes it clear that the practice was firmly established.

works so hard and so constantly that even beasts of burden would scarcely endure it; and this work of theirs is so necessary that no commonwealth could survive for a year without it? Yet they earn so meagre a living and lead such miserable lives that beasts would really seem to be better off. Beasts do not have to work every minute, and their food is not much worse; in fact they like it better, and besides, they do not have to worry about their future. But work-ingmen must not only sweat and suffer without present reward, but agonise over the prospect of a penniless old age. Their daily wage is inadequate even for present needs, so there is no possible chance of their saving for their declining years.

Now isn't this an unjust and ungrateful commonwealth? It lavishes rich rewards on so-called gentry, loan sharks, and the rest of that crew, who don't work at all or are mere parasites, purveyors of empty pleasures. And yet it makes no provision whatever for the wel-fare of farmers and colliers, labourers, carters and carpenters, with-out whom the commonwealth would simply cease to exist. After society has taken the labour of their best years, when they are worn out by age, sickness and utter destitution, then the thankless com-monwealth, forgetting all their pains and services, throws them out to die a miserable death. What is worse, the rich constantly try to grind out of the poor part of their meagre pittance, not only by pri-vate swindling but by public laws. It is basically unjust that people who deserve most from the commonwealth should receive least. But now they have distorted and debased the right even further by giving their extortion the form of law; and thus they have palmed injustice off as legal.[114] When I run over in my mind the various common-wealths flourishing today, so help me God, I can see in them nothing *Reader, note well!* but a conspiracy of the rich, who are fattening up their own interests under the name and title of the commonwealth.[115] They invent ways and means to hang on to whatever they have acquired by sharp prac-tice, and then they scheme to oppress the poor by buying up their toil and labour as cheaply as possible. These devices become law as soon

---

[114] Russell Ames suggests that there is a particular reference to legislation of recent Par-liaments, completed in 1515, 'which re-enacted the old statutes against laborers while removing clauses unfavorable to employers' (*Citizen Thomas More and His Utopia* (Princeton, 1949), p. 128).

[115] Many readers have seen an allusion here to the judgement of St Augustine: 'if justice is left out, what are kingdoms but great robber bands?' (*The City of God* IV.iv).

as the rich, speaking through the commonwealth – which, of course, includes the poor as well – say they must be observed.

And yet when these insatiably greedy and evil men have divided among themselves goods which would have sufficed for the entire people, how far they remain from the happiness of the Utopian Republic, which has abolished not only money but with it greed! What a mass of trouble was cut away by that one step! What a thicket of crimes was uprooted! Everyone knows that if money were abolished, fraud, theft, robbery, quarrels, brawls, seditions, murders, treasons, poisonings and a whole set of crimes which are avenged but not prevented by the hangman would at once die out. If money disappeared, so would fear, anxiety, worry, toil and sleepless nights. Even poverty, which seems to need money more than anything else, would vanish if money were entirely done away with.

Consider if you will this example. Take a barren year of failed harvests, when many thousands of men have been carried off by hunger. If at the end of the famine the barns of the rich were searched, I dare say positively enough grain would be found in them to have kept all those who died of starvation and disease from even realising that a shortage ever existed – if only it had been divided equally among them. So easily might men get the necessities of life if that cursed money, which is supposed to provide access to them, were not in fact the only barrier to our getting what we need to live. Even the rich, I'm sure, understand this. They must know that it's better to have enough of what we really need than an abundance of superfluities, much better to escape from our many present troubles than to be burdened with great masses of wealth. And in fact I have no doubt that every man's perception of where his true interest lies, along with the authority of Christ our Saviour (whose wisdom could not fail to recognise the best, and whose goodness would not fail to counsel it), would long ago have brought the whole world to adopt Utopian laws, were it not for one single monster, the prime plague and begetter of all others – I mean Pride. *A striking phrase*

Pride measures her advantages not by what she has but by what other people lack. Pride would not deign even to be made a goddess if there were no wretches for her to sneer at and domineer over. Her good fortune is dazzling only by contrast with the miseries of others, her riches are valuable only as they torment and tantalise the poverty of others. Pride is a serpent from hell that twines itself around the hearts of men, acting like a suckfish[116] to hold them back from choosing a better way of life.

Pride is too deeply fixed in human nature to be easily plucked out. So I am glad that the Utopians at least have been lucky enough to achieve this republic which I wish all mankind would imitate. The institutions they have adopted have made their community most happy and, as far as anyone can tell, capable of lasting forever. Now that they have torn up the seeds of ambition and faction at home, along with most other vices, they are in no danger from internal strife, which alone has been the ruin of many other nations that seemed secure. As long as they preserve harmony at home, and keep their institutions healthy, the Utopians can never be overcome or even shaken by their envious neighbours, who have often attempted their ruin, but always in vain.

*

When Raphael had finished his story, I was left thinking that quite a few of the laws and customs he had described as existing among the Utopians were really absurd. These included their methods of waging war, their religious practices, as well as others of their customs; but my chief objection was to the basis of their whole system, that is, their communal living and their moneyless economy. This one thing alone utterly subverts all the nobility, magnificence, splendour and majesty which (in the popular view) are the true ornaments and glory of any commonwealth. But I saw Raphael was tired with talking, and I was not sure he could take contradiction in these matters, particularly when I recalled what he had said about certain counsellors who were afraid they might not appear knowing enough unless they found something to criticise in other men's ideas. So with praise for the Utopian way of life and his account of it, I took him by the hand and led him in to supper. But first I said that we would find some other time for thinking of these matters more deeply, and for talking them over in more detail. And I still hope such an opportunity will present itself some day.

Meantime, while I can hardly agree with everything he said (though he is a man of unquestionable learning and enormous

---

[116] The remora has a suction plate atop its head, by which it attaches itself to the underbelly of larger fish or the hulls of ships. Impressed by the tenacity of its grip, the ancients fabled that it could impede ships in their course.

experience of human affairs), yet I freely confess that in the Utopian commonwealth there are many features that in our own societies I would like rather than expect to see.

END OF BOOK II.

THE END OF THE AFTERNOON DISCOURSE OF
RAPHAEL HYTHLODAY ON THE LAWS AND
INSTITUTIONS OF THE ISLAND OF UTOPIA,
HITHERTO KNOWN TO BUT FEW, AS
RECORDED BY THE MOST
DISTINGUISHED AND LEARNED MAN,
MR THOMAS MORE,
CITIZEN AND SHERIFF OF LONDON.

Ancillary materials from
the early editions

THOMAS MORE TO HIS FRIEND PETER GILES,
WARMEST GREETINGS[1]

My dear Peter, I was absolutely delighted with the judgement of that very sharp fellow you recall, who posed this dilemma regarding my *Utopia*. – If the story is offered as fact (says he) then I see a number of absurdities in it; but if it is fiction, then I think More's usual good judgement is wanting in some matters. – I'm much obliged to this man, whoever he may be (I suspect he is learned, and I see he's a friend). His frank judgement gratified me more than any other reaction I've seen since my book appeared. First of all, led on by fondness either for me or for the work itself, he did not give up in the middle, but read my book all the way through. And he didn't read carelessly or quickly, as priests read their hourly prayers – those who read the hours at all – but slowly and carefully in order to consider the different points thoughtfully. Then, having selected certain elements to criticise, and not very many of them, he says that he approves, not rashly but deliberately, of all the rest. Finally, he implies in his very words of criticism higher praise than those who set out to compliment the book on purpose. For he shows clearly how well he thinks of me when he expresses disappointment in a

---

[1] This second letter of More to Giles appeared only in the 1517 edition, where it immediately followed the text of Book II. The identity of the 'very sharp fellow' (below) is unknown – if indeed More didn't invent him.

passage that doesn't read as clearly as it should – whereas I would think myself lucky if I had been able to set down just a few things out of many that were not altogether absurd.

Still, if I in my turn can deal as frankly with him as he with me, I don't see why he should think himself so acute (or, as the Greeks say, so sharp-sighted) just because he has noted some absurdities in the customs of the Utopians, or caught me putting forth some half-baked ideas about the constitution of their republic. Aren't there any absurdities elsewhere in the world? And don't other philosophers, when they describe a society, a ruler, or a pattern of private life, sometimes say things that won't hold up? Actually, if it weren't for the great respect I retain for certain highly distinguished names, I could easily produce a number of philosophical notions which I can hardly doubt would be universally condemned as absurd.

But when he questions whether the book is fact or fiction, I find *his* judgement quite awry. There's no denying that if I had decided to write of a commonwealth, and a tale of this sort had come to my mind, I might not have shrunk from a fiction through which the truth, like medicine smeared with honey, might enter the mind a little more pleasantly. But I would certainly have softened the fiction a little, so that, while imposing on vulgar ignorance, I gave hints to the more learned which would enable them to see through the pretence. And so if I had merely given such names to the ruler, the river, the city and the island as would indicate to the knowing reader that the island was nowhere, the city a phantom, the river waterless and the prince without a people,[2] that would have made the point. It wouldn't have been hard to do, and would have been far more clever than what I actually did. If the veracity of a historian had not actually required me to do so, I am not so stupid as to have preferred those barbarous and meaningless names of Utopia, Anyder, Amaurot and Ademos.

But I see, my dear Giles, some men are so suspicious that in their circumspect sagacity they can hardly be brought to believe what we simple-minded and credulous fellows wrote down of Hythloday's story. My personal credibility among these people may be shaken, not to speak of my reputation as a historian. So I am glad I can say of my brainchild what Mysis, in Terence's play, says about

---

[2] This is of course precisely what the names mean.

Glycerium's boy, whose legitimacy was in question: 'By all the gods, I am glad that some ladies of rank were present at his birth.'[3] Similarly, it's my good fortune that Raphael told his story, not just to you and me, but to a great many other men, of the utmost gravity and unquestioned probity. I don't know whether he told them more and greater things, but I'm sure he told them nothing less than he told us.

If the doubters are not satisfied even with these witnesses, let them consult Hythloday himself, for he is still alive. I recently heard from some travellers out of Portugal that as late as last March he was still healthy and vigorous as ever. Let them get the truth out of him, let them put him to the question and drag it forth. I only want them to understand that I answer only for my own work, not for anyone else's credit. Farewell to you, my dear Peter, to your charming wife and clever little daughter – to all, my wife sends her very best wishes.

ERASMUS OF ROTTERDAM TO JOHANN FROBEN HIS BELOVED GOSSIP, GREETINGS[4]

While heretofore I have always thought extremely well of my friend More's writings, yet I rather mistrusted my own judgement because of the very close friendship between us. But when I see all the learned unanimously subscribe to my opinion, and praise even more highly than I the divine wit of this man, not because they love him better but because they see more deeply into his merits, I must speak from a full heart, and no longer shrink from saying openly what I feel. How would his fortunate disposition have stood forth if his

---

[3] *The Lady of Andros* IV.iv; ll. 770–1.

[4] In a letter of *c.* 20 September 1516, More told Erasmus that he was anxious that *Utopia* 'be handsomely set off with the highest of recommendations, if possible, from several people, both intellectuals and distinguished statesmen' (*Selected Letters*, p. 76). Erasmus complied, in spades. The practice of publishing books with buttressing commendations was common then as now, but the amount of ancillary material in *Utopia* is unusual. This and the following letters, poems and other materials are given in the order in which they appear in the edition of March 1518. Most of them preceded the text, but three items were printed at the end.

It is interesting that Erasmus' own tribute – which implies some reservations – did not appear until this third edition of the book. The addressee, Johann Froben (*c.* 1460–1527), was the distinguished printer whose Basel shop produced the edition and its November successor. He was Erasmus' 'gossip' ('god-sib') because Erasmus was god-father to his infant son.

genius had been nurtured in Italy![5] If he had devoted his whole
energy to the service of the Muses, maturing gradually, as it were,
towards his own proper harvest! As a youth, he toyed with epigrams,
many written when he was only a boy. He has never left Britain
except a couple of times to serve his prince as an ambassador to
Flanders.[6] Apart from the cares of a married man and the respon-
sibilities of domesticity, apart from his official post and floods of
legal cases, he is distracted by so many and such important matters
of state business that you would marvel he finds any free time at all
for books.

For this reason I am sending you his *Youthful Exercises*[7] and his
Utopia, so that, if you think proper, their appearance under your
imprint may commend them to the world and to posterity. For the
authority of your firm is such that a book is sure of pleasing the
learned as soon as it is known to issue from the house of Froben.
Farewell to you, to your excellent father-in-law,[8] your dear wife,
and your delightful children. Make sure that Erasmus, the little son
we share in common, and who was born among books, is educated
in the best of them.

Louvain, 25 August 1517

WILLIAM BUDE TO THOMAS LUPSET OF ENGLAND, GREETINGS[9]

Most learned of young men, Lupset, you have left me enormously in
your debt by presenting me with the *Utopia* of Thomas More, and

---

[5] I.e., in the centre of humanist learning.

[6] Actually More had visited the Universities of Louvain and Paris in 1508 (see *Selected Letters*, p. 17). The Flanders missions were the one in which he began *Utopia* (1515), and another in 1517.

[7] The *Youthful Exercises (Progymnasmata)* were a series of rival translations by More and the grammarian William Lily: both men made Latin versions of the same Greek epigrams. The *Exercises* were bound with *Utopia* in the Froben editions, along with a second series of epigrams by More and some by Erasmus.

[8] Wolfgang Lachner, a bookseller who played an important part in Froben's business.

[9] While studying in Paris in 1517, Thomas Lupset (*c.* 1498–1530) supervised the printing of two of Thomas Linacre's translations of works by Galen (the great medical author-ity of classical Greece), and of the second edition of *Utopia*. He also made the acquaintance of Guillaume Budé (1468–1540), the foremost French humanist of the time.

thereby introducing me to an extremely amusing and potentially profitable book. In fact, you had already asked me to do what on my own account I was more than ready to do – that is, to read over the six books of Galen, *On Protecting One's Health*, which Doctor Thomas Linacre, a man equally skilled in both languages, lately turned from Greek to Latin. He has bestowed on his original so generous a gift of his own elegant Latinity that if all the works of this author (who alone, in my view, comprehends the whole science of medicine) were turned into such Latin, the medical profession would be bound to suffer much less in future from its ignorance of Greek.

Your lending to me for so long a time the manuscripts of Linacre was an act of the highest generosity; I profited immensely from my first hasty reading of them, and promise myself even richer rewards from study of the printed volume which you are just now busily ushering through the presses of Paris. On these scores I already thought myself sufficiently in your debt; and now, as an appendix or supplement to your former gift, you send me the *Utopia* of More, a man of the keenest wit, the most agreeable temper and the most profound experience in judging human affairs.

I took his book with me to the country, and kept it in my hands as I bustled about, in constant activity, supervising the various workmen (for you no doubt know, or have at least heard, that for more than a year now I have been absorbed in business connected with my country house); but I was so fascinated with learning about and reflecting on the customs of the Utopians that I almost forgot and even dismissed entirely the management of my household affairs. What nonsense, I thought, is all this bustle over getting and saving, this whole business of constantly accumulating more and more!

And yet this appetite, like a hidden parasite rooted in our flesh from birth, preys on the whole human race – there is no one who does not recognise that fact. I might almost say we are bound to admit that this is the real end of the legal profession, as well as of all the arts and disciplines of government: to make each man act with ingrained and calculated malice towards the neighbour with whom not only civil law but fellow-feeling should unite him. He is always about grabbing something, taking it away, extorting it, suing for it, squeezing it out, breaking it loose, gouging it away, ripping it off, snatching it, snitching it, filching it, pinching it, pilfering it, getting away with it – partly with the tacit complicity of the laws, partly with their direct sanction, he carries off what he wants and makes it his own.

This is particularly frequent in those countries where the two codes of law, called civil and canon, exercise their double jurisdiction. Everyone knows that through their precedents and institutions the opinion has solidified that only men skilled in the ways – or perhaps just the wiles – of the law, only artists of the legal phrase or fraud, contrivers of complicated contracts, fosterers or festerers of litigation – vultures to the common man, exponents of a perverse, confused and unjust justice – only such men as these are to be thought the high priests of equity and right. They only are qualified to say peremptorily what is just and good, they only are fit to decide (a much greater matter) what each and every man should have, what he should not have, how much he can have and how long he can keep it. Yet such a delirious arrangement as this has been accepted by public opinion.

Because they are short-sighted almost to blindness, most men tend to think an individual has received full justice to the extent that he has satisfied the requirements of the law or received what the law allots him. But if we measured our rights by the norm of truth and the prescriptions of the naked gospel, nobody is so dull or senseless as not to recognise enormous differences. God's law is as remote from the justice dispensed by canonical regulation, and real equity is as distant from what is expressed through civil courts and royal decrees, as the rule, established by Christ, founder of our human condition, and observed by his disciples, is distant from the decrees and regulations of those who think the perfection of human happiness and the ultimate good are to be found in the gold-bags of Croesus and Midas.[10] So that if you now mean by justice what it used to mean in days gone by, that is, the power which gives to each his due, you must either conclude it has no public existence at all, or that it acts (excuse the expression) like a mere kitchen-maid. And this is true whether you regard the behaviour of our modern rulers or the relations between our fellow citizens and fellow countrymen.

Of course some argue that our modern law derives from an ancient and authentic code (which they venture to call the law of nature), according to which the stronger a man is the more goods he should have, and the more goods he has the more power he should

---

[10] Proverbial rich men of antiquity.

exercise over his fellow citizens.[11] The result of this logic is that it is now an accepted principle of the law of nations that men who are of no practical use whatever to their fellow citizens – so long as they can keep everyone else tied up in contractual knots and complicated testamentary clauses (matters which appear to the ignorant multitude, no less than to those humanistic scholars who live as retired and disinterested seekers after truth, as a vulgar combination of Gordian-knot tricks and common charlatanry) – such men, it is now agreed, should have each one an income equal to a thousand ordinary citizens, equal to a whole city, or even more. And naturally they also acquire impressive titles, as of honourable men, munificent men, pillars of society. This happens in every age and climate, under any institutions and among any peoples who have decided that a man should have supreme power and authority in the degree that he has built up the biggest possible private fortune for himself and his heirs. And the process is cumulative, since his descendants and their descendants strive to build up their inheritance by one gigantic increment after another – meanwhile cutting off stringently all their connections, relatives and close kinfolk.

But the founder and controller of all property, Christ, left his followers a Pythagorean rule of mutual charity and community property; not only so, but he confirmed it unmistakably when Ananias was sentenced to death for violating the rule of community property.[12] By this arrangement, Christ seems to me to have undermined – at least among his own disciples – all that body of civil and canon law recently worked out in so many vast volumes. Yet this is the law which we see now holding the fort of jurisprudence, and ruling over our destinies.

The island of Utopia, however, which I hear is also called Udepo-

---

[11] The idea that there is an unchanging, universally valid body of natural law, which men apprehend by reason and instinct, was a central concept of legal and political theory from classical antiquity to the nineteenth century. Since the equality of men was normally regarded as a fundamental precept of natural law, the doctrine that might makes right could be derived only from a perverse understanding of it. The 'law of nations' (below) signifies the body of legal principles common to different peoples: what is universally practised, but not necessarily consonant with natural justice. For a clear exposition of the development and relationship of these concepts, see R. W. Carlyle and A. J. Carlyle, *A History of Mediaeval Political Theory in the West*, 3rd edn, 1 (London, 1930), especially 33–44.

[12] Pythagoras was believed to have instituted a communal life among his followers. On the communism of the early Christians, see Acts 2:44–5. When Ananias sold a possession and 'kept back part of the price', Peter reproached him and he fell dead (Acts 5: 1–5).

tia,[13] is said (if the story is to be believed) still to preserve, by mar-vellous good fortune, access both in its public and its private life to the truly Christian customs and the authentic wisdom. It has done so by holding tenaciously to three divine institutions: absolute equality of all good and evil things among the citizens (or, if you prefer, the sharing of them among all the citizens on a basis of absolute equal-ity); a fixed and unwavering dedication to peace and tranquillity; and utter contempt for gold and silver. These three principles suf-fice to defeat all swindles, impostures, tricks, wiles and under-handed deceptions. Would that the gods, by their divine power, could cause these three pillars of Utopian policy to be fixed by the bolts of strong and settled conviction in the minds of all mortal men. You would promptly witness the withering away of pride, greed, idiot competition and almost all the other deadly weapons of our hellish adversary. The immense weight of all those legal volumes, which occupy brilliant and solid minds for their whole lifetimes, would suddenly turn to empty air, the paper food for worms or used to wrap parcels in shops.

By all the gods above, I wonder what special holiness protected the Utopians, so that their island alone was shielded for so many centuries from the assaults, either stealthy or violent, of avarice and cupidity? What prevented those enemies from driving out justice and modesty under an onslaught of shameless effrontery? Would that God, in his infinite goodness, had dealt as kindly with those regions which still keep and proudly proclaim their allegiance to the faith called by his most holy name! Surely avarice, the vice which now depraves and debases so many keen and vigorous minds, would then depart forever, and the golden age of Saturn[14] would return to earth. One might even think that Aratus and the other old poets were mistaken when they said Astraea, goddess of Justice, had fled the earth and taken refuge in her constellation in the zodiac.[15] For if Hythloday is right she must have been here all along, on the island of Utopia, and not in heaven at all, yet.

In fact, I have decided, after investigating the matter, that Utopia lies outside the bounds of the known world. Perhaps it is one of the

---

[13] From Greek *oudepote*, 'never'.

[14] Saturn ruled over the first and best of the mythological four ages of man, an era of peace and happiness that ended when he was deposed by his son Jupiter.

[15] According to the Greek poet Aratus (fl. third century BC), Astraea, who is identified with the constellation Virgo, departed earth in the face of mounting human wicked-ness.

Fortunate Isles,[16] near neighbour to the Elysian Fields. As More himself says, Hythloday has not yet told exactly where it is to be found. Though it is divided into a number of different cities, they are all united or confederated in a single society named Hagnopolis,[17] a nation content with its own customs and possessions, blessedly innocent, leading its own exalted life – lower than heaven, indeed, but far above the smoke and stir of our familiar world, which – among men's constant squabbles, as violent as they are silly – is being swept down a whirling cataract to the abyss.

Our knowledge of this island we owe to Thomas More, who in our time made known this model of the happy life and rule for living well. The actual discovery he attributes to Hythloday; the substance of the book is all his. Thus, if Hythloday is the architect of the Utopian nation, the founder of its customs and institutions from which he has brought home and fashioned for us the very pattern of a happy life, More is its adorner, who has bestowed on the island and its holy institutions the grace of his style, the polish of his diction. He it is who has shaped the city of the Hagnopolitans to the standard of a model and a general rule, and added all those touches which give beauty, order and authority to a magnificent work. And yet he claims as his part of the task only the role of a humble artisan. Evidently he made scruple of asserting too great a role in the book, lest Hythloday have grounds for complaint that More had pre-empted the glory due to him, which he might have had if he himself had chosen to write up his travels. *He feared, of course, that Hythloday, who was living of his own free will on the island of Udepotia, might some day return, and be angry that More had left him only the husks of credit for his discovery, having taken the best part for himself. Such consideration is characteristic of wise and virtuous men.*[18]

While More himself is a man of weight whose word carries great authority, I am bound to give him full credit on the word of Peter Giles of Antwerp. Though I do not know Giles personally – apart from commendations that have reached me of his learning and character – I love him because he is the sworn and intimate friend of

---

[16] In classical culture, the Fortunate Isles, or Islands of the Blest, were the eternal paradise of heroes. They were thought to be situated – like Utopia – in the remotest west. The Isles were sometimes loosely identified with the Elysian Fields, that part of Hades where the virtuous pass eternity in the favourite pursuits of their former lives.

[17] Holy City, or City of the Saints.

[18] Budé wrote the italicised passage in Greek.

Erasmus, a most distinguished man who has contributed so much to every sort of literary study, whether sacred or profane. With him I have long been in correspondence, with him I have long been on terms of close friendship.

Farewell, my dearest Lupset, and as soon as you can convey my greetings, whether in person or by letter, to Linacre, that pillar of the British name in all that concerns good learning; by now, I hope, he is no more yours than ours. He is one of the very few men whose good opinion I should be glad, if possible, to earn. When he was here, he made the very deepest and most favourable impression on me and on Jean Du Ruel, my friend and fellow student.[19] His excellent learning and careful diligence I shall always be one of the first to admire and strive to imitate.

Give my best regards also to More, either by letter, as I said before, or in person. He is a man whose name, in my opinion, and as I have often said, stands high in the ledgers of Minerva;[20] I particularly love and revere him for what he has written about this island of the New World, Utopia. Our own age and ages to come will discover in his narrative a seedbed, so to speak, of elegant and useful concepts from which men will be able to borrow practices to be introduced into their own several nations and adapted for use there. Farewell.

Paris, 31 July [1517]

SIX LINES ON THE ISLAND OF UTOPIA
WRITTEN BY ANEMOLIUS,[21]
POET LAUREATE,
AND NEPHEW TO HYTHLODAY BY HIS SISTER

> 'No-Place' was once my name, I lay so far;
> But now with Plato's state I can compare,
> Perhaps outdo her (for what he only drew
> In empty words I have made live anew
> In men and deeds, as well as splendid laws):
> 'The Good Place'[22] they should call me, with good cause.

[19] Like Linacre, Du Ruel was a physician and translator.

[20] The Roman goddess of wisdom and the arts, identified with the Greek goddess Athena.

[21] From Greek *anemolios*, 'windy'. The real author of the poem is not known.

[22] The word translated here is *Eutopia*, from Greek *eu-* ('happy', 'fortunate') plus *topos* ('place').

MAP OF THE ISLAND OF UTOPIA[23]

[23] The map is the work of the Dutch painter Ambrosius Holbein, brother of the much better-known Hans Holbein the Younger. The 1516 edition had a cruder map, by an unknown hand.

THE UTOPIAN ALPHABET[24]

a b c d e f g h i k l m n o p q r s t u x y
Ò⊖⊕⊙⊖⊕⊚⊋⋐⋒⋓⊛△⅃Ⴑ⌐⌐⌐◻▣▥⅊⊟⊡

A QUATRAIN IN THE UTOPIAN LANGUAGE

Vtopos   ha   Boccas   peula   chama.
Bargol   he   maglomi   baccan
foma   gymnofophaon
Agrama   gymnofophon   labarem
bacha   bodamilomin
Voluala   barchin   heman   la
lauoluola   dramme   pagloni.

A LITERAL TRANSLATION OF THESE VERSES

Utopus it was who redrew the map,
And made me an island instead of a cape:
Alone among nations resplendent I stand,
Making virtue as plain as the back of your hand –
Displaying to all without argumentation
The shape of a true philosophical nation.
Profusely to all of my own store I give;
What is shown me that's better, I gladly receive.

[24] Peter Giles was evidently responsible for this page (see p. 125). The sample of the Utopian language, which reveals affinities with Greek and Latin, has enough internal consistency to suggest it was worked out with some care. See the discussion in *CW*, IV, 277–8. The Utopian quatrain is followed by a stilted Latin 'translation', which we have translated into stilted English.

TO THE MOST DISTINGUISHED MASTER
JEROME BUSLEYDEN
PROVOST OF AIRE, AND COUNCILLOR
TO THE CATHOLIC KING CHARLES,
PETER GILES OF ANTWERP SENDS GREETINGS[25]

Most eminent Busleyden, the other day Thomas More (who, as you very well know from your intimate acquaintance with him, is one of the great ornaments of our age) sent me his *Island of Utopia*. It is a place known so far to only a few men, but which should be studied by everyone, as going far beyond Plato's Republic. It is particularly interesting because it has been so vividly described, so carefully discussed and so acutely analysed by a man of such great eloquence. As often as I read it, I seem to see even more than I heard from the actual words of Raphael Hythloday – for I was present at his discourse, along with More. As a matter of fact, Hythloday himself showed no mean gifts of expression in setting forth his topic; it was perfectly plain that he wasn't just repeating what he had heard from other people, but was describing exactly what he had seen close at hand with his own eyes and experienced in his own person, over a long period of time. I consider him a man with more knowledge of nations, peoples and business than even the famous Ulysses. Such a man as this has not, I think, been born in the last eight hundred years; by comparison with him, Vespucci seems to have seen nothing at all. Apart from the fact that we naturally describe what we have seen better than what we have only heard about, the man had a particular skill in explaining the details of a subject. And yet when I contemplate the same matters as sketched by More's pen, I am so affected by them that I sometimes seem to be living in Utopia itself. I can scarcely believe, by heaven, that Raphael saw as much in the five

[25] This letter dedicates *Utopia* to Busleyden and also gives Giles a chance to talk about the book and his own role in its creation. The Burgundian Busleyden (*c.* 1470–1517) was a prominent statesman and patron of learning. His dignities included the office of Provost of St Peter's Church at Aire and membership in the council of Charles, Prince of Castile, who inherited the title 'the Catholic' (along with the throne of Aragon) at the death of his grandfather Ferdinand II in 1516. More met Busleyden in 1515 and wrote three flattering epigrams about him and his fine house. He was particularly interested in having an opinion of *Utopia* from Busleyden, whom he regarded as ideally combining learning, virtue and practical experience (*Selected Letters*, pp. 80, 76). For Busleyden's commendation of *Utopia*, see pp. 126–9.

years he lived on the island as can be seen in More's description. That description contains, in every part of it, so many wonders that I don't know what to marvel at first or most. Perhaps it should be the accuracy of his splendid memory, which could recite almost word for word so many different things that he had heard only once; or else perhaps his good judgement, which traced back to sources of which the common man is completely ignorant the evils that arise in commonwealths and the blessings that could arise in them. Or finally I might marvel at the nerve and fluency of his language, in which, while preserving a pure Latin style, he has expressed incisively and comprehensively a great many matters of important policy. This is all the more remarkable in a man distracted, as he is, by a mass of public business and private concerns. But of course none of these remarks will surprise you, most erudite Busleyden, since you have already learned from your intimate acquaintance with him to appreciate the more-than-human, the almost-divine genius of the man.

For the rest, I can add nothing to what he has written. There is, indeed, a little scrap of verse, written in the Utopian tongue, which Hythloday showed to me after More had gone away. I've prefixed to it an alphabet of the Utopian language, and also added to the volume a few little marginal notes.[26]

As for More's difficulties about locating the island, Raphael did not try in any way to suppress that information, but he mentioned it only briefly and in passing, as if saving it for another occasion. And then an unlucky accident caused both of us to miss what he said. For while Raphael was speaking of it, one of More's servants came in to whisper something in his ear; and though I was listening, for that very reason, more intently than ever, one of the company, who I suppose had caught cold on shipboard, coughed so loudly that some of Raphael's words escaped me. But I will never rest till I have full information on this point, not just the general position of the island, but its exact latitude – provided only our friend Hythloday is safe and alive.

For we hear various stories about him, some people asserting that he died on the way home, others that he got home but didn't like the

---

[26] Giles here seems to claim credit for the marginal glosses in *Utopia*. On the title page of the 1517 edition, however, they are attributed to Erasmus. Perhaps both contributed glosses; or perhaps the 1517 edition (in which neither was involved) is wrong.

way things were going there, retained his old hankering for Utopia, and so made his way back to that part of the world.[27]

It's true, of course, that the name of this island is not to be found among the cosmographers, but Hythloday himself had a simple answer for that. For, he said, either the name that the ancients gave it has changed over the ages, or else they never discovered the island at all. Nowadays we find all sorts of lands turning up that the old geographers never mentioned. But what's the point of piling up these arguments authenticating the story, when we already have it on the word of More himself?

His uncertainty about having the book published I attribute to his modesty, and very creditable it is. But on many scores, it seems to me a work that should not be suppressed any longer; on the contrary, it eminently deserves to be sent forth into the hands of men, especially under the powerful protection of your name. Nobody knows More's good qualities better than you do, and no man is better suited than you to serve the commonwealth with good counsels. At this work you have laboured for many years, earning the highest praise for wisdom as well as integrity. Farewell, then, you Maecenas[28] of learning and ornament of our era.

Antwerp, 1 November 1516

JEROME BUSLEYDEN TO THOMAS MORE, GREETINGS[29]

For you, my most distinguished friend More, it was not enough to have devoted all your care, labour and energy to the interest and advantage of individuals: such is your goodness and liberality that you must bestow them on the public at large. You saw that this goodness of yours, however great it might be, would deserve more favour, achieve higher renown, and aim at greater glory, the more widely it was diffused, the more people shared in it and were bene-

---

[27] Cf. More's second letter to Giles, which says (p. 114) that Hythloday is alive and well and living in Portugal.

[28] Maecenas was the patron of Virgil, Horace and other Roman writers; and is often, as here, the type of the patron.

[29] This and the two following items appeared as prefatory materials in the 1516 edition. For the editions of 1517 and 1518, they were moved to the back of the book. On Busleyden, see p. 124n. This letter came directly to Erasmus, who had solicited it, with a covering note making it clear that Busleyden wrote out of esteem for Erasmus (*CWE*, iv, 483). Like Budé, the wealthy Busleyden singles out Utopian communism for special praise.

fited by it. This is what you've always tried to do on other occasions, and now by a singular stroke of luck you've attained it again – I mean by that afternoon's discussion which you've described and now published, about something that everyone must envy, the right and proper constitution of the Utopian Republic.

It is a delightful description of a wonderful establishment, replete with profound erudition and a consummate knowledge of human affairs. Both qualities meet in this work so equally and so congenially that neither yields to the other, but both contend on an even footing. You enjoy such a wide range of learning and such profound experience that whatever you write comes from full experience, and whatever decisions you take carry a full weight of learning. A rare and wonderful happiness! And all the more remarkable in that it withdraws itself from the multitude and imparts itself only to the few – to such, above all, as have the candour to wish, the erudition to understand, the public trust to put into practice and the authority to judge in the common interest as honourably, accurately and practically as you do now. For you clearly don't consider yourself born for yourself alone, but for the whole world; and so by this splendid work you have undertaken to place the whole world in your debt.

You could hardly have accomplished this end more effectually and correctly than by setting before rational men this pattern of a commonwealth, this model and perfect image of proper conduct. And the world has never seen a model more perfect than yours, more soundly established or more desirable. It far surpasses the many celebrated commonwealths of which so much has been said, those of Sparta, Athens and Rome. Had they been founded under the same auspices as your commonwealth, with the same institutions, laws, regulations and customs, certainly they would not now be lying flat, level with the ground and extinguished – alas! – beyond all hope of rebirth. On the contrary, they would now be intact, fortunate and prosperous, leading a happy existence – mistresses of the world, besides, and dividing a far-flung empire, by land and by sea.

Feeling pity for the wretched fate of these commonwealths, you feared lest others, which now hold supreme power, should undergo the same fate; so you drew the portrait of a perfect commonwealth, one which devoted its energies less to setting up perfect laws than to forming the very best men to administer them. And in this they were absolutely right; for without good rulers, even the best laws (if we take Plato's word for it)[30] would be nothing but dead letters. Such rulers as these serve above all as models of probity, specimens of good conduct, images of justice and patterns of virtue for the guidance of any well-established commonwealth. What is needed is prudence in the rulers, courage in the military, temperance in the private citizenry, and justice among all men.[31]

Since the nation you praise so lavishly is clearly formed on these principles, no wonder if it seems not only a challenge to other nations but an object of reverence to all the peoples, and an achievement to be celebrated among future generations. Its great strength lies in the fact that all squabbles over private property are removed and no one has anything of his own. Within the society all men have everything in common, and thus every action and each decision, whether public or private, trifling or important, is not directed by the greed of the many or the lusts of the few, but aims at upholding a single uniform rule of justice, equality and community solidarity. All things being thus tightly bound to a single aim, there is necessarily a clean sweep of everything that might serve as torch, kindling, or fuel for the fires of intrigue, luxury, envy and wrong. These are vices into which even decent men are sometimes pushed against their will, and to their own incomparable loss, by private property or lust for gain or that most pitiful of emotions, ambition. From these sources explode quarrels, clashes and wars worse than civil,[32] which not only overthrow the flourishing state of supremely happy republics, but cause their previous glories, their past triumphs, rich prizes and proud spoils taken from defeated enemies to be utterly defaced.

If my thoughts on this point should be less than absolutely convincing, only consider the swarm of perfectly reliable witnesses I can call to my support – I mean the many great cities destroyed, the states crushed, the republics beaten down, the towns burnt up. Not only have they disappeared with scarcely a trace – not even their names are preserved by any history, however far back it reaches.

Such terrible downfalls, devastations, disasters and other calamities of war our future commonwealths (if we have any) will be able to

[30] E.g., *Laws* VI.751B–C.
[31] Prudence (or wisdom), courage, temperance and justice are the four Cardinal Virtues of Greek and Roman ethics. Busleyden's remark summarises the main argument of Book IV of the *Republic* (especially 427D–434C).
[32] 'Wars worse than civil' is the opening phrase of Lucan's *Pharsalia*, an epic poem on the civil war between Pompey and Caesar.

escape only if they adapt themselves to the Utopian pattern and don't swerve from it, as people say, by a hair's breadth. If they act so, the result will fully convince them how much they have profited by the service you have done them; especially since, by your help, they will have learned to keep their republic healthy, unharmed and victorious. Their debt to you will be no less than that owed to a man who has saved not just one citizen of a country, but the entire country itself, from danger.

Farewell for now. May you continue to prosper, ever contriving, carrying out and completing new plans which will bring long life to your country, and to yourself immortality. Farewell, most learned and humane More, supreme ornament of your Britain and of this world of ours.

From my house at Mechlin, 1516

ON UTOPIA BY GERARD GELDENHOUWER[33]

If pleasure you seek, good reader, it's here;
If profit, no book is more suited to teach;
If both – on this island, both will appear
To sharpen at once both your thoughts and your speech:
Here the springs both of good and of ill are set forth
By More, London's star of incomparable worth.

TO THE READER BY CORNELIS DE SCHRIJVER[34]

You seek new monsters from the world new-found?
New ways of life, drawing on different springs?
The source of human virtue? The profound
Evil abyss? The void beneath all things?
Read here what's traced by More's ingenious pen,
More, London's pride, and Britain's first of men.

---

[33] The Dutch humanist Geldenhouwer (1482–1542) assisted the printer Dirk Martens in the production of many books, including the first edition of *Utopia*.

[34] De Schrijver, a Latin poet of wide reputation, settled in Antwerp by 1515, where he became a close associate of Peter Giles.

BEATUS RHENANUS TO WILLIBALD PIRCKHEIMER, COUNSELLOR TO THE EMPEROR MAXIMILIAN AND SENATOR OF NUREMBERG, GREETINGS[35]

... Well, just as these toys[36] serve to display More's wit and notable erudition, so the keenness of his judgement in matters of business comes brilliantly clear in *Utopia*. Concerning which I need say only a few passing words because the book has already been praised as it deserves in a resounding preface by that most rigorous of scholars Budé, who is an incomparable exponent of the higher learning, as well as a giant, even unique, genius of French letters. More's book contains principles of a sort not to be found in Plato, Aristotle, or even in the Pandects of your favourite Justinian.[37] Its teachings are perhaps less philosophical than those others, but they are more Christian. And yet (if you'd like to hear, with the favour of the Muses, a good story), when the subject of *Utopia* came up here lately in a gathering of various important people, and when I praised it, one foolish fellow said More deserved no more credit than a paid scribe, who simply writes down what other people say after the fashion of a recording secretary (so they call him), who may sit in a meeting, but expresses no ideas of his own. Everything in the book, he said, came from the mouth of Hythloday; all More did was write it down. And for that More deserved no more credit than attaches to making a good transcript. And there were actually people in the group who gave this simpleton high marks as a man of shrewd insights. *Now, don't you admire the sly wit of More, who can bamboozle men like these, not just ordinary dolts but men of standing and trained theologians at that?* ...[38]

Basel, 23 February 1518

---

[35] The son of a Rheinau butcher named Bild, Beatus Rhenanus (1485–1547), like other humanists, took a new Latin name to go with his classical learning. Under this cheerful sobriquet ('Beatus' means 'happy', 'blessed') he assisted Erasmus in the publication of many of his works, in addition to pursuing scholarly enterprises of his own. He supervised the printing of the 1518 editions of *Utopia*, which also included epigrams by More, William Lily and Erasmus, and supplied this dedicatory epistle, of which we print only the part dealing with *Utopia*.

[36] I.e., the epigrams.

[37] The Pandects or Digests of Roman law were compiled under the Emperor Justinian in the sixth century AD.

[38] The italicised sentence is in Greek.

JEAN DESMAREZ OF CASSEL TO MASTER PETER GILES, GREETINGS[39]

I have read the *Utopia* of your friend More, along with his *Epigrams* – whether with more pleasure or admiration, I do not know. How happy is Britain, which now blossoms forth with talents of such eminence that they rival those of antiquity! And how lumpish are we,[40] duller than lead, if we cannot be roused to compete for the same sort of praise by examples so near at hand. 'It is shameful to keep silent', says Aristotle, 'while Isocrates still speaks.'[41] We should feel disgraced to devote ourselves only to pleasure-seeking and money-making, when the British, who live at the ends of the earth, are bringing forth, thanks to the generosity of their princes, learning in such profusion. Although the Greeks and Italians used to have almost a monopoly of good learning, Spain too had some eminent names to vaunt among the ancients; Scythia, savage though she was, had her Anacharsis;[42] Denmark her Saxo Grammaticus; France her Budé. Germany has many men famous for learning, England even more, and those among the most distinguished. For what must we think of the others, if More is so outstanding – and this despite his youth, the distraction of his many other public and private concerns,[43] and the fact that literature is far from his primary vocation? Only we, of all people, seem satisfied to scratch our skins and stuff our moneybags. Indeed, even we are shaking off our torpor and preparing to take part in this glorious contest, in which it is no shame to be beaten and splendid to be victorious. Many examples provoke us to it, in every direction; so does our admirable Prince Charles,[44] who rewards nothing more generously than learning,

---

[39] Desmarez (d. 1526) was public orator and professor at the University of Louvain. His letter and poem (below) appeared among the prefatory materials in the editions of 1516 and 1517. Erasmus was not deterred by his long friendship with Desmarez from authorising Beatus Rhenanus to omit both productions from the 1518 editions (*CWE*, v, 229).

[40] I.e., we of the Low Countries.

[41] The remark, which is attributed to Aristotle by Quintilian (*The Education of the Orator* III.i.14), paraphrases a line in Euripides' lost play *Philoctetes*. Isocrates was the pre-eminent orator of Aristotle's time.

[42] Anacharsis (fl. sixth century BC) was a Scythian sage, famed less for his wisdom than for the fact that, among the Scythians, any sage was conspicuous. Saxo Grammaticus (fl. thirteenth century) wrote *Gesta Danorum*, a history of his native land.

[43] This phrase, which seems to be adapted from a very similar one in Giles' letter to Busleyden (p. 125), is one of several instances of the derivative nature of Desmarez' letter.

[44] Prince Charles of Castile.

while the great Maecenas and patron of all good pursuits, Jean Le Sauvage, Chancellor Burgundy, also urges us forward.

Let me warmly encourage you, most learned Peter Giles, to have *Utopia* published as soon as possible; in it can be seen, as in a mirror, everything that relates to the proper establishment of a commonwealth. I could wish that, just as the Utopians have begun to accept our religion, we might adopt their system of ordering society. The change might easily be made if a number of distinguished and persuasive theologians were sent to Utopia; they would invigorate the faith of Christ, which has already taken root there, and then on their return bring to us the customs and institutions of the islanders.

Utopia owes a great debt to Hythloday for making known this land which ought not to have remained obscure; it owes an even greater debt to the acute More, whose skilful pencil has drawn it for us so vividly. In addition to both of them, not the least part of the thanks must be directed to you, who are making public both Hythloday's conversation and More's report of it – to the no small delight of future readers, and their even greater profit, if they weigh prudently the various elements of the tale.

Utopia has so stirred my spirit that, though long a stranger to the Muses, I have invoked them anew[45] – with what success you must be the judge.

Fare you well, most courteous Peter Giles, you who are both practitioner and patron of good letters.

From my house at Louvain, 1 December [1516]

Poem on the new island of Utopia by the Same John Desmarez, Orator of the University of Louvain

The men of Rome were brave; the lofty Greeks
Famous for eloquence; Sparta's men were strict;
The Germans, tough; the honest Marseillais
Noted for probity; urbane and witty men
Flourished in Attica; Africans were deep.
France bred religious saints; the British men
Were world-wide famous for munificence.

The virtues have their special homes; what here
Abounds is somewhere else in short supply.
Only one isle, Utopia, displays to men
The sum of all the virtues in one place.

[45] I.e., in the following verses.

Index[1]

[1] Chronology and Suggestions for further reading are not indexed. Utopian ideas, attitudes, customs and institutions are indexed under 'Utopia (the country)'.

Index

Index

Index

virtue (contd)
   religion 95, 98, 105; Utopian views
   on xxv, 67, 69–71, 75, 76, 84, 89, 99, 102

war xxvi, 14, 15, 16–18, 29–31, 43, 56,
   87–95, 103, 128

Wind, Edgar xxin., 68n.
women: see Utopia: women in

Zapoletes xxvi, 90–2

CAMBRIDGE TEXTS IN
THE HISTORY OF POLITICAL THOUGHT

Titles published in the series thus far

KNOX *On Rebellion* (edited by Roger A. Mason)

LAWSON *Politica sacra et civilis* (edited by Conal Condren)

LEIBNIZ *Political Writings* (edited by Patrick Riley)

LOCKE *Two Treatises of Government* (edited by Peter Laslett)

LOYSEAU *A Treatise of Orders and Plain Dignities* (edited by Howell A. Lloyd)

Luther and Calvin on Secular Authority (edited by Harro Höpfl)

MACHIAVELLI *The Prince* (edited by Quentin Skinner and Russell Prince)

MALTHUS *An Essay on the Principle of Population* (edited by Donald Winch)

MARSIGLIO OF PADUA *Defensor minor* and *De translatione Imperii* (edited by Cary Nederman)

MARX *Early Political Writings* (edited by Joseph O'Malley)

JAMES MILL *Political Writings* (edited by Terence Ball)

J. S. MILL *On Liberty*, with *The Subjection of Women* and *Chapters on Socialism* (edited by Stefan Collini)

MILTON *Political Writings* (edited by Martin Dzelzainis)

MONTESQUIEU *The Spirit of the Laws* (edited by Anne M. Cohler, Basia Carolyn Miller and Harold Samuel Stone)

MORE *Utopia* (edited by George M. Logan and Robert M. Adams)

NICHOLAS OF CUSA *The Catholic Concordance* (edited by Paul E. Sigmund)

NIETZSCHE *On the Genealogy of Morality* (edited by Keith Ansell Pearson)

PAINE *Political Writings* (edited by Bruce Kuklick)

PRICE *Political Writings* (edited by D. O. Thomas)

PRIESTLEY *Political Writings* (edited by Peter Miller)

PROUDHON *What is Property?* (edited by Donald R. Kelley and Bonnie G. Smith)

PUFENDORF *On the Duty of Man and Citizen according to Natural Law* (edited by James Tully)

The Radical Reformation (edited by Michael G. Baylor)

HERBERT SPENCER *The Man versus the State* and *The Proper Sphere of Government* (edited by John Offer)

Utopias of the British Enlightenment (edited by Gregory Claeys)

VITORIA *Political Writings* (edited by Anthony Pagden and Jeremy Lawrence)

VOLTAIRE *Political Writings* (edited by David Williams)

WEBER *Political Writings* (edited by Peter Lassman and Ronald Speirs)

WILLIAM OF OCKHAM *A Short Discourse on Tyrannical Government* (edited by A. S. McGrade and John Kilcullen)